THE
GROWTH OF
SOCIOLOGICAL
THEORIES

THE GROWTH OF SOCIOLOGICAL THEORIES

DAVID G. WAGNER

 SAGE PUBLICATIONS Beverly Hills London New Delhi

Copyright © 1984 by Sage Publications, Inc.

For information address:

SAGE Publications, Inc.
275 South Beverly Drive
Beverly Hills, California 90212

SAGE Publications India Pvt. Ltd.
C-236 Defence Colony
New Delhi 110 024, India

SAGE Publications Ltd
28 Banner Street
London EC1Y 8QE, England

Printed in the United States of America

Library of Congress Cataloging in Publication Data

Wagner, David G. (David George), 1949-
    The growth of sociological theories.

    Bibliography: p.
    1. Sociology. I. Title.
HM24.W18   1984   301'.01   84-8376
ISBN 0-8039-2332-5

FIRST PRINTING

Contents

Acknowledgments

If writing a book is a humbling experience, writing a book on the analysis of sociological theory is doubly or trebly so. I have never been so aware of the extent of my own ignorance, of the tremendous complexity of the issues involved, as in my work here.

Perhaps for this reason, many sociologists seem to believe that serious consideration of theoretical issues like these is best left until much later in one's career—or even left to the "elder statesmen" of the discipline. It is specifically in opposition to this attitude that I have developed the ideas in this book, for it is my belief that theoretical analysis and expertise is as essential to the performance of *any* sociological work as is methodological analysis and expertise. Theoretical analysis is the responsibility of *all* sociologists at *any* stage in their careers, not the province of a few esteemed colleagues.

This view is certainly not new with me. Anyone trained in the Department of Sociology at Stanford University is exposed to this position; extensive practice in theoretical analysis is a basic part of every student's training, regardless of specialty. I am exceedingly grateful to have been a part of that program, and am indebted to both the faculty and graduate students at Stanford, who provide a social and intellectual climate that greatly facilitates such work.

I am particularly indebted to Joseph Berger, whose course on theoretical analysis first interested me in the issues I consider in this book. Both on my dissertation and in my subsequent career, his insights, criticisms and "positive unit evaluations" have been essential to the development of my sociological identity. His fertile intellect has been a source of stimulation for all who have worked with him over the past twenty-five years; I am privileged to have been one of those so honored.

The advice and support of "Buzz" Zelditch has also been of great help to me. I particularly cherish his admonition to "trust" my intellectual instincts—to worry only about whether *I* believe I am learning something.

7

At Iowa Ed Lawler has been quite valuable in helping me put together the ideas in this book. He has been unstinting in his willingness to accept interruptions in his office, in the hall, or at lunch, to discuss a new example I wished to use or a new way of presenting an idea I wished to consider. Our discussions have been long and interesting. I hope they have been as fruitful for him as they have been for me.

Students in my graduate course in sociological theory probably have heard me express the ideas in this book at greater length and in greater detail than has anyone else. They have been especially helpful in forcing me to say exactly what I mean. Although I appreciate all (well, almost all) of the suggestions my students have given me, I have profited most from the comments of Marcia Radosevich, Derek Mason, and Becky and Tom Ford. May their students be as stimulating.

Several people have read the entire manuscript, or major parts of it. The comments of Jonathan Turner, Dave Willer, and, again, Ed Lawler, have been quite valuable.

The good people at Sage have been very friendly, cooperative, and helpful. They have even provided recovery service for a lost wallet at the ASA meetings in Detroit.

Rose Garfinkle prepared all the figures in this book. She did a highly professional job, including translating my often obscure instructions flawlessly.

Every treatise I have ever read has expressed great appreciation for the aid and support of at least one family member, usually a spouse. The acknowledgement is so standard it has always seemed perfunctory to me. I know now that I was wrong. I could not have survived either intellectually or emotionally without the regular support and encouragement of my wife, Nancy. She has shared both the triumphs and the tribulations, the former with an excitement that prolongs the "high" and the latter with a sensibility and an equanimity that overcomes the "low." I could never have written the book without her help.

Finally, I cannot let pass without mention the aid of a collection of inanimate objects. This book was composed at a terminal connected to the IBM 3033 at the University of Iowa using the Wylbur text editor and Syspub text formatter. Computer composition not only has dramatically reduced the time required to make revisions, it has helped me clarify my thinking as I write. I highly recommend the new word processing technologies.

Chapter 1

Introduction

ISSUES TO BE CONSIDERED

This book is about the cumulativeness of sociological knowledge. The subject is a matter of extensive debate in sociology. Almost everyone has staked out a position on one side of the issue or another. For example, there are some sociologists who see cumulative growth as an essential characteristic of a sociological science (e.g., Parsons, 1954; Freese, 1980). Others, following Kuhn, see such growth as a deception; changes in scientific knowledge are generally revolutionary and nonprogressive (e.g., Ritzer, 1975; Bernstein, 1978).[1] Still others treat the natural sciences separately from the social sciences. Theoretical change is seen as generally progressive in the natural sciences, where the subject matter is assumed to be nonreactive and observation to be objective. In contrast, theoretical change cannot be progressive in the social sciences, where the subject matter is quite reactive and observation heavily value-laden (e.g., Gouldner, 1970; Winch, 1958).

Ironically, despite strong differences of opinion regarding the possibility of cumulative growth in sociology, there is little disagreement about the *reality* of such growth. The consensus seems to be that little or no growth has occurred. Certainly, none of the sources I have cited sees sociological knowledge as progressive to any significant degree. Many others concur (e.g., Bergner, 1981; Alexander, 1982).

I do not. I believe that cumulative theoretical growth is possible and that it occurs with some frequency in contemporary sociology. However, we often fail to see that growth because we have an inadequate, one-dimensional view of what it means for sociological knowledge to be cumulative. My

AUTHOR'S NOTE: *The five "situation" diagrams used in this chapter are reprinted from* Arthur Stinchcombe, Constructing Social Theories. *Copyright © 1969 by Harcourt Brace Jovanovich, Inc. Reprinted by permission.*

purpose in writing this book, then, is to present a more adequate multidimensional view of cumulativeness (and, incidentally, to demonstrate the reality of cumulative growth in sociology with the illustrations I use).

In the presentation of any view of cumulative growth, at least three closely related issues seem to be involved. First is our understanding of the criteria with which our more systematic knowledge claims—theories—are assessed: How do we determine whether or not our claims are justified? The second issue concerns the criteria by which theory choices are made: How do we determine which of our claims should be retained and which rejected? Our responses to these two issues then help to determine our response to the third issue, involving the possibilities of theory growth: Do our claims improve over time in any way and, if so, how do they improve?

The most comprehensive and detailed consideration of these issues has occurred since about 1965 in texts and monographs on theory construction. (See, for example, Blalock, 1969; Boudon, 1974; Chafetz, 1978; Dubin, 1978; Gibbs, 1972; Glaser and Strauss, 1967; Hage, 1972; Mullins, 1971; Reynolds, 1971; Stinchcombe, 1968; Wallace, 1971; Zetterberg, 1965.) Traditionally, and with few exceptions, these works have assumed that empirical support is the primary criterion of theory assessment, that on the basis of relative empirical support those theories could be selected which are more likely to be true and, hence, that the growth of theoretical knowledge could be described as a cumulative approximation of empirical sociological truth.

I believe that this view of cumulative growth is inadequate, that all three issues involve more than the relationship between theory and observation. Specifically, I claim that all three issues involve relationships between theories, as well as relationships between theory and observation. Put another way, I argue that theory assessment, choice, and growth all must be analyzed within a context of related theories. Cumulativeness, then, must be evaluated in terms of theoretical context, not just in terms of empirical context.

I develop this argument in several ways: (1) by elaborating some of the ways in which theories may be related to each other, thereby generating distinct types of theoretical context, (2) by specifying the differential implications of these types for theory assessment, choice, and growth, and (3) by proposing a systematic framework for analyzing (and pursuing) cumulative theory development that takes theoretical context into account.

Let us consider first, however, the character of the more traditional analysis and the problems in it that I attempt to resolve.

AN EXAMPLE OF THE TRADITIONAL VIEW
OF CUMULATIVENESS IN SOCIOLOGY

In his text *Constructing Social Theories*, Arthur Stinchcombe presented a series of inference situations that he considered illustrative of "the basic logical process of science." Basically, this process involves the following steps:

(1) the statement of a theory,

(2) the derivation of one or more empirical statements from the theory, using operational definitions of theoretical concepts,

(3) the performance of one or more empirical investigations, testing the derived statements, and

(4) the assessment of the credibility of the theory (i.e., the probability that it is true), given the outcomes of the empirical investigations.

The simplest situation arises when an investigation indicates that an empirical consequence of the theory is false. Under these circumstances the theory must also be false; it therefore must be rejected. Suppose, using Stinchcombe's example, we are concerned with Durkheim's theory of egoistic suicide, stated simply as "A higher degree of individualism in a social group causes a higher rate of suicide in that group" (Stinchcombe, 1968: 15). If individualism is defined in terms of the degree to which behavior is determined by one's self (rather than by norms enforced by others), empirical statements can be derived predicting higher rates of suicide in groups whose members' conduct is less closely regulated by the group. For instance, Protestants—presumably less closely regulated than Catholics—should have a higher suicide rate than Catholics. If an empirical investigation indicates that, in fact, Catholics have a higher rate than Protestants, then the theory is false by logical implication and must be rejected.

This argument can be stated somewhat more concisely and much more abstractly using Stinchcombe's format:

Situation I

$$A \rightarrow B$$

B false

A false

where A represents the proposed theory, B represents an empirical consequence of the theory, the arrow represents implication, and the line
separating the premises from the conclusion represents logical derivation.[2]
Theory A implies empirical consequence B. However, investigation shows
consequence B to be false. Therefore, A is also false.

But what is our assessment of theory A if consequence B is shown to
be true? In the example, how do we evaluate Durkheim's theory if Protestants do have higher suicide rates than Catholics? Stinchcombe argues
we may by logical deduction consider A, the theory, "more credible"—
symbolically,

Situation II

$$A \rightarrow B$$

B true

A more credible

Furthermore, if several similar implications of A are shown to be true, A
is that much more credible:

Situation III

$$A \rightarrow B(1), \ B(2), \ B(3)$$

B(1), B(2), B(3) all true

A substantially more credible

Thus, if investigations show that Protestants have higher suicide rates than
Catholics in France—B(1)— *and* in Germany—B(2)—*and* in Austria—
B(3)—then, by logical deduction, Durkheim's theory of egoistic suicide is
"substantially more credible."[3]

Credibility can be enhanced even further, Stinchcombe suggests, if the
empirical derivations to be tested are quite different (i.e., if there is very
little "overlap" among the theories that imply each derivation). A is but
one of the number of theories from which it is possible to derive any particular empirical consequence. If all of the tested consequences are similar,
few if any of the alternatives to A can be rejected as clearly false. However,
the more dissimilar the derivations from A are, the less likely it is that the

alternative theories will permit all the same derivations. If the derivations are all supported, then those alternatives that did not permit all the derivations can be rejected.

Suppose we derive predictions about suicide rates among Protestants and Catholics only in France, not in all three countries; then we derive a thoroughly different prediction that married Frenchmen with children should have a lower suicide rate than bachelor Frenchmen (since presumably families provide a degree of external normative control of behavior not present for bachelors). While some theories (e.g., of religion) may permit derivation of suicide rates for Protestants and Catholics in any number of countries, few such theories are likely also to permit derivation of suicide rates based on marital status. Thus, if our investigations show support for both the "religion" and "marital status" derivations from Durkheim's theory, any alternative theory that is concerned with religion alone or marital status alone can be ruled out (via Situation I). Durkheim's theory is made even more credible, since more of its potential competitors have been ruled out.

In Stinchcombe's more abstract form this situation can be represented as follows. Assume that alternatives to theory A include (but are not limited to) C, D, E, F, Q, R, S, and T. Then,

Situation IV

$A \rightarrow B(1), B(n)$

$B(1), B(n)$ very different

$C, R \rightarrow$ not $B(1)$

$D, E \rightarrow$ not $B(n)$

$B(1), B(n)$ true

C, R, D and E false

A (and F, Q, S and T) remain

A much more credible

Of course, Situation IV still fails to establish A as the only possible theoretical explanation, since theories F, Q, S, and T are equally credible (although Stinchcombe does not note this in his discussion). Unfortunately, since the number of potential alternative theories is indefinite, no inference situation can establish A's truth so clearly. However, Stinchcombe argues, a reasonably close approximation can be achieved in Situation V, the crucial experiment. In this situation, contradictory empirical conse-quences of A and the *most* likely alternative are tested. If testing shows the derivation from the most likely alternative to be false, that theory can be rejected and A becomes very much more credible.

Thus, a theory of mental illness might be the most likely alternative to Durkheim's theory. One obvious derivation from the illness theory might be that rates of suicide and of mental illness should be highly correlated. By contrast, Durkheim's theory would imply no significant correlation be-tween the two rates. If investigation shows little or no correlation of rates, then Durkheim's theory is made even more credible, since its most likely competitor has been ruled out. In more abstract form,

Situation V

A or C or (D, E, ...)

(D, E, ...) unlikely

A → B(j)

C → not B(j)

B(j) true

C false

A (or D, E, ...) [(D, E, ...) unlikely]

A very much more credible

Thus, in general, (1) the more empirical consequences of a theory that are supported by observations, (2) the greater the variety of the consequences supported, and (3) the more frequently those consequences are contradic-tory to the consequences of the most likely alternative theories, the more credible the original theory becomes. While no observations can establish a theory definitively as true, by these methods it is possible to arrive at a theory that is increasingly more probable than its alternatives—and closer to the truth.

ANALYSIS OF THE
TRADITIONAL VIEW

Stinchcombe's analysis of "the logical process of science" is a remarkably clear exposition of what is probably the most prevalent view of theory assessment, choice, and growth in sociology today. First, *theory assessment* is almost exclusively a process of comparing individual theories (or more precisely, in Stinchcombe's terms, derivations from such theories) with observations. The value of a theory is determined by its empirical support. If observations support (i.e., are consistent with) the derivations from the theory, the theory is true, or at least credible. In addition, the more frequent, the more varied, and the more discriminating the support, the greater is the truth content (credibility) of the theory. But if any observations do not support (i.e., are inconsistent with) the derivations, the theory is false; it has no truth content, no credibility whatever.

Second, *theory choice* is based almost exlusively on the outcomes of these comparisons of theory with observations. Those theories that are supported empirically are accepted as more credible; they are selected *because* they are assumed to be closer to the truth. Conversely, theories that are falsified by empirical evaluation are rejected as noncredible. They are straightforwardly false on the grounds of logical contradiction.

Finally, *theory growth* is directly related to the theory choices (hence, to the theory assessments) made. Theory assessment is based primarily on observational criteria (i.e., whether the theory accounts for the observations or not); theory choice is based on a comparison of the outcomes of those assessments (i.e., which theory accounts for more observations). Thus, theory growth consists of the accumulation of observations in support of a theory. In other words, the primary characteristic of theory growth in the traditional view is increasing empirical support.

Such a view does *not* require that growth occur, that supporting observations accumulate. If empirical investigations fail to discriminate sufficiently among the derivations of alternative theories, theory assessment labels these alternatives as equally credible; therefore, no theory choice takes place; therefore, theory growth does not occur.

Furthermore, empirical investigations may fail to support any of the alternative theories; in such a case, all the candidate theories are assessed as false, all are rejected, and again growth does not occur. Of course, if no empirical investigations are performed, no assessments can be made at all; theory choice and growth are not even at issue. Thus, this view claims only that *if* theory growth occurs, it can be described as a cumulative approximation of empirical truth. If growth does not occur, it may be because the alternative theories are all supported, or all rejected, or even ignored.

CRITICISM OF THE TRADITIONAL VIEW

In many ways the traditional sociological view, as exemplified by Stinch-combe's variant, is a valuable and informative one. It recognizes empirical evaluation as an essential element in the assessment of scientific theories, sociological or otherwise. It emphasizes the importance of falsification as a component of that assessment process. It illustrates clearly the value of multiple and diverse empirical assessments of theories. It provides decision rules for theory choice based on such assessments. Finally, it specifies a process by which our theoretical knowledge can grow.

However, several problems limit the usefulness of this view. Consider first issues of theory assessment. The assessment situations considered by Stinchcombe are all straightforward and unambiguous; observations either support or do not support particular empirical derivations. But the assessment situations that occur in sociological research are usually somewhat less clear than that. Observations may be inconsistent with each other, thus yielding contradictory judgments of the support for a derivation. Observations may be consistent with the direction of relationship predicted by the derivation (i.e., positive or negative) but inconsistent with the predicted form (e.g., linear or curvilinear). Observations may even be consistent in both direction and form but only within a specified range. In all such cases the assessment situation is more complex than is allowed by most variants of the traditional view. Frequently, observational support or nonsupport of empirical derivations cannot be clearly established; therefore, the theories tested by these observations cannot be assessed as clearly true or clearly false.

Some variants of the traditional view propose statistical criteria (e.g., proportion of explained variance, probability of a Type I error) to resolve some of the more ambiguous cases. But even these proposals are limited by the untimely arbitrary choice of a threshold value for the significance or importance of observational support for a derivation.

However sophisticated the procedures proposed, most are designed to deal with one type of evaluation—the consistency of observation statements with theoretical statements (i.e., empirical support). But theories are often evaluated on criteria other than empirical support. Range (the number of different problems for which an account is provided), scope (the comprehensiveness of the account of a *particular* problem), precision, and rigor of theoretical structure are among the more important of these criteria.

Usually sociological theorists make some effort to discuss at least a few of these criteria. For example, Stinchcombe's section on "levels of generality in social theory" (Stinchcombe, 1968: 47-53) is a somewhat oblique consideration of scope as a criterion of assessment. Such discussions are seldom as complete and as detailed as they should be. Certainly no work in theory or theory construction in sociology of which I am aware provides the kind of exposition of any of these criteria that Stinchcombe provides for the criterion of empirical support. Nor has anyone considered the consequences of conflicting assessments based on different criteria—say, when one theory has greater scope but is less precise and another theory is quite precise but has much narrower scope. The traditional view does not even consider such situations.

Consider now issues of theory choice. The view represented by Stinchcombe argues for the rejection of any theory assessed as false via the criterion of empirical support. But some theories have not been rejected despite numerous refutations. Perhaps the best example of this phenomenon is Merton's (1938) theory of social structure and anomie, which continues to be chosen as a "credible" alternative in deviance despite several negative assessments (see, e.g., Hyman, 1953; Hirschi, 1969; Kornhauser, 1978). Another example is Festinger's (1957) theory of cognitive dissonance (with negative assessments by Chapanis and Chapanis, 1964; Gerard and Mathewson, 1966; Aronson, 1969; Bem, 1972). Of course, these examples might all be dismissed as aberrations; their persistence may be explained on "extra-scientific" grounds like individual or class-based values and ideologies.

Unfortunately, the problem is more basic than the occasional acceptance of false theories. Something more complex than the simple acceptance or rejection of theories seems to occur. Suppose, for example, that a theory has been supported by observations; the theory is then accepted as credible. But the process of theory construction and evaluation does not always end at this point. Modifications may be introduced in the theory that, for example, permit the derivation of more precise predictions. The revised theory would probably then be retested with new observations. The process may continue indefinitely with each revision leading to retesting and each new evaluation leading to further revision. Technically, each revision creates a new theory; yet the theory that is replaced was accepted, not rejected; there is no reason for it to be displaced. Views like Stinchcombe's can include such theories only as alternatives to the credible theory, alternatives that have not yet been falsified. This means of inclusion seems to ignore much of the special character of theories so closely related to the credible theory, as well as the reasons behind their construction.

The problem occurs as well when theories evaluated as false are considered. A theory that is false should be rejected, according to the traditional view. But again, the process of theory construction and evaluation often does not end at this point. A theory may be evaluated as false for a myriad reasons other than a general and basic inadequacy of its account of some empirical phenomenon. Indicators of key concepts may have been poorly chosen; the scope of the theory may have been ill-defined; the observational situation may not have been clearly established as within the scope of the theory (especially if the theory's scope is not stated clearly or explicitly); one key assumption may have been wrong, or poorly formulated, or inconsistent with the rest of the theory. The list of possibilities is very large. In short, it is not necessary that an entire theory be inadequate for an evaluation of "false" to occur. It is quite reasonable, therefore, to modify a falsified theory rather than to reject it. Each modification constitutes an attempt to eliminate some possible inadequacies of the falsified theory while retaining most of its virtues. The revised theory (again, technically, a new theory) may then be retested and supported, or falsified and further revised. Again the process may continue indefinitely, although at some point the bulk of negative evidence may come to outweigh the worth of further investigation, and the theory may be evaluated more or less permanently as false.

The problem extends still further. The traditional view requires that *all* theories assessed as false be rejected. Thus, if observations fail to support the derivations of any reasonable alternative, none of the alternatives should be credible enough to be accepted. Yet, in a great many cases, a theory clearly false in some respects may be retained *if there is no better alternative*. It seems clear then that Stinchcombe's analysis of theory choice (and its variants) ignores many of the more frequent choice situations. The only decision rules for theory choice that are ordinarily specified are those which apply to quite unambiguous and consistent assessment situations, and even there the rules are often broken.

Finally, with regard to theory growth, the traditional view in sociology considers only changes that are associated with changes in the empirical support of a theory. But, as I have suggested, there are several other criteria besides empirical support that are used in the assessment of theory. The choice situations that arise from these assessments are frequently more complex than the traditional view allows, sometimes even involving the acceptance of a theory known to be false. It seems reasonable to assume, then, that the character of theory growth may also be somewhat more complex. While the accumulation of observations in support of a theory is certainly an important aspect of theory growth, it is not the only basis upon which growth may be based; increases in rigor, precision, scope, and range are also relevant. Most important, growth may still occur in the absence of increasing observational support. Theorizing is a creative enterprise. Developing a theory often depends on going "beyond" the available evidence into new and uncharted territory. If theory growth were to depend entirely on increasing observational support, no new ideas or theories would be possible.

To review, the more important limitations of the traditional view in sociology involve the inadequacy of its accounts of (1) assessments involving criteria other than empirical support, (2) choice situations more ambiguous than the straightforward acceptance or rejection of a theory, and (3) theory growth in the absence of, or in combination with, increasing empirical support.

Sociologists are probably aware of most, if not all, of these limitations. Three kinds of responses seem likely. First, some might argue that the traditional view is intended to be normative and not descriptive; it shows how theoretical activity should proceed if it is to be scientific, not how it actually does proceed. Thus, the degree to which actual activity matches the description given by the traditional view is not a measure of the adequacy of that view, but of the scientific sophistication of the discipline. This response ignores an important problem. Most would agree that criteria like rigor and precision should be used in assessing theories (although they may not agree on which criteria are most important or on how the criteria should be applied). Thus, there is at least one aspect of the normative analysis that is incomplete. Unfortunately, that incompleteness has ramifications throughout the analysis, as noted in my criticisms. Even if the traditional view is intended only to be normative, it is still incomplete; a further analysis remains to be done that considers the application of assessment criteria other than empirical support.

Others might respond that, whether or not the traditional view is intended also to be normative, the description it provides must be abstract. Since the analysis is concerned with the assessment, choice, and growth of theories in general, it is impossible for it to describe those processes completely for any single theory concretely. It is the price we must pay if we wish to develop general knowledge. But there is nothing in this response that excuses us from the responsibility to improve our description on an abstract level. In the traditional view there are large areas of ambiguity in the analysis of all three areas of theoretical activity, as noted. Clearly, it would be valuable to attempt to clear up some of these ambiguities.

Finally, some (notably sociologists of science and knowledge) might argue that discrepancies between the arguments of the traditional view and actual theoretical activity indicate the operation of external social processes. If, for example, a theory remains credible even after it has been consistently falsified, that may not indicate an inadequacy in the traditional view so much as it indicates the presence of some sociological factor, such as the ideological support the theory may provide for a dominant social class. I would certainly not deny the importance of sociological factors in theoretical activity. However, it is a questionable practice to define the domain of application of a process as "residual" (i.e., that which is left unexplained by other processes is subject to explanation by this process); in fact, I will argue in Chapter 6 that sociological factors should affect *all* theoretical activity, not just that which is discrepant with the traditional view. Further, unless one is willing to argue that intellectual processes have no force in human affairs, both internal (intellectual) and external (sociological) processes should affect theoretical activity throughout its full range. Just as external factors should provide some explanation of activity consistent with the traditional view, internal factors should provide some explanation of activity inconsistent with the traditional view. Thus, the presence of external sociological factors in theoretical activity is not an excuse for the absence of an attempt to improve the internal explanations of that activity. It remains a useful task to attempt to resolve some of the problems in the traditional view that I have outlined, while retaining what appears to be of value in that view.

SOURCES OF INADEQUACY IN
THE TRADITIONAL VIEW

Most of the problems I have discussed seem to be related to the failure of the traditional view to focus sufficient attention on the context of other related theories within which assessment, choice, and growth appear to occur.

For example, assessment outcomes seem frequently to depend on what alternative theories are available for comparison. Thus, a candidate theory

A may be consistent with more observations than an alternative theory B, but with fewer observations than a second alternative C. If theory A is compared with theory B alone, it will be evaluated as more credible or probable than B; but if theory A is compared with theory C, it will be evaluated as false. The *same evidence* leads to opposite assessments, depending on the context within which the comparison is made.

The same contextual effect also occurs frequently with other criteria of assessment. A judgment of the precision of a theory may depend on whether the theory is more precise or less precise than its alternatives. If the theory is more precise than some alternatives and less precise than others, opposite evaluations will result, depending on which alternatives are available for comparison.

Even theories for which there are no substantive alternatives may be assessed in comparison with at least one other alternative—the theory that the operation of the phenomenon under study is statistically random. It would seem useful, therefore, to explore the consequences for theory assessment of comparison with alternative theories under varying circumstances. Of particular interest would be circumstances involving criteria of assessment other than, or in addition to, empirical support. It would also be useful to explore differences in assessment situations depending on whether or not the comparison theories are related closely to the candidate theory (e.g., when one theory is actually a revision of another); different, or different combinations of, criteria of assessment are likely to be involved. If these explanations are fruitful, some of the more ambiguous assessment situations left unanalyzed in the traditional view may be more clearly understood.

Problems in the traditional account of theory choice seem also to depend, at least in part, on the context of related theories. First, of course, if assessment involves more than one criterion, the decision as to which of two or more theories to accept or reject is more difficult. A candidate theory may be more precise, but of lesser scope, than its alternative. It is not immediately obvious which theory should be retained and which discarded. Nor is it clear which theory is to be preferred if one derivation from the candidate theory has just been falsified by observations, while all the derivations of its alternative—with much narrower scope, far less precise predictions, and considerably less rigorous theoretical structure—have been supported by those same observations. In each of these cases the choice to be made depends on the evaluation over two or more criteria of *both* theories.

Second, the presence of theories related in some way to the candidate theory may suggest a third kind of theory choice, namely modification. Suppose, for example, that the candidate theory has been clearly assessed as false. Suppose also that another theory using an almost identical theoretical structure of concepts and assertions, but slightly less precise in its predictions, has been supported empirically. It is unlikely that the candidate theory will be discarded; rather, most of the theoretical structure held in common with the other theory will probably be retained, a modification made in the concepts or assertions that affect the theory's precision, and the theory retested. In the absence of that other related theory, the candidate theory would be much more likely to be rejected outright. Thus, the effect of even a clear assessment of a theory as false may depend on whether it is closely related to other theories or not.

Again, it would appear useful to explore the effect of other related theories on the translation of assessment outcomes into choice decisions, and on the character and consequences of those decisions.

The character of theory growth may also be related to the comparisons of one theory with its alternatives or variants, not only to the comparison of that theory with observations. Certainly, if theory assessment and theory choice are affected by theoretical context as I have suggested, theory growth will also be affected as a direct consequence of the assessments and choices made. The character of growth would be seen to be rather more complex, involving changes in rigor, precision, scope, or range (for example), as well as in empirical support. Progress in one area—say, scope—may be at the expense of retrogression in another—say, precision—depending on the comparison theories. Furthermore, the accumulation of observations in support of a theory, though necessary, may not be sufficient to establish its credibility. Other, perhaps less well-supported theories, may be preferred if comparisons indicate they are more favorably assessed on criteria like rigor or scope.

Differences in the assessment and choice processes for more and less closely related alternative theories may also influence the character of growth. For example, if a particular structural relationship among a set of theories encourages modification rather than rejection of a falsified theory in the set, then such theories may remain acceptable longer; the progress toward greater empirical support may be slowed while advances are made that are based on modifications in other areas. Of course, the character of growth may be still further complicated if different types of modifications (e.g., changes in scope) also affect theory assessment and choice differently. There may be many characteristic patterns of growth, depending on how theories are related.

Once more it is likely that an exploration of the effect of various theoretical relationships (or their absence) on the analysis of theory growth would be useful.

THE WORK TO BE DONE

In short, an investigation of the theoretical contexts in which theoretical activity occurs may contribute to (1) a more precise understanding of the criteria by which theories are assessed, (2) a more comprehensive enumeration of potential assessment situations and their consequences for theory choice, (3) a more complete specification of possible choice decisions and their influence on the character of growth, and (4) a more discriminating analysis of patterns of theory growth than is presently possible using the traditional sociological view. Therefore, in the chapters that follow I initiate an investigation of the context of related theories within which I have suggested that theory assessment, choice and growth occur.

My first concern is with defining my unit of analysis. Just what is a "theory"? Unfortunately, the term is a particularly elusive one in sociology; it has been used to refer to so many different kinds of work. Little wonder then that our understanding of assessment, choice, and growth is poor, given the trouble we have in identifying exactly what it is that is being assessed, is chosen, and grows. Consequently, in Chapter 2 I explicate two of the most basic meanings of the term "theory," suggest some important differences between them, and limit my focus to one of those meanings for most of the rest of the discussion.

With this clarification in focus it is possible to consider the issue of theoretical context directly in Chapters 3 and 4. The bulk of Chapter 3 is concerned with elaborating and exemplifying five different types of theoretical context. The implications of each of these contexts for assessment, choice, and growth are then developed in Chapter 4. The overall conclusion I draw from this work is that theory development is a much more complex, *multidimensional* process than is generally assumed.

The complexity of theory development demands a more consciously directive effort at the task. Therefore, in Chapter 5 I discuss a systematic framework for developing theories in terms of *theoretical research programs*. Pursuit of such programs, I argue, is likely to enhance our ability to build cumulative knowledge in sociology.

In Chapter 6 I consider some of the ways in which social factors impinge on our attempts to build cumulative knowledge programmatically. I show first how the entire enterprise is framed by metatheoretical assumptions and then how social factors influence our choice of metatheory. The analysis demonstrates that social factors are critical in determining whether one theory or another has the opportunity to grow, while internal intellectual factors are critical in determining whether or not growth actually occurs.

All of these are then brought together in Chapter 7, where I present some preliminary guidelines for the formulation of a full-fledged theory of theory growth. The model I propose is evolutionary in character and draws heavily on the work of Popper, Kuhn, Lakatos, and Toulmin in the philosophy of science.

Finally, in a concluding chapter I use my analysis to suggest some ways in which our thinking about the role of theory and theorizing in sociology ought to be revised.

Chapter 2

What Is A Theory?

THE PROBLEM

In Chapter 1 I identified a number of flaws in the traditional view of theory assessment, choice, and growth in sociology, as exemplified in the work of Stinchcombe (1968). In fact, there is at least one additional flaw in the traditional view, again exemplified in Stinchcombe's work.

Basically, the flaw involves the rather vague and simplistic understanding we sociologists have of the term "theory." Consider Stinchcombe's analysis. In all of his inference situations a single letter—say, A—is used to represent an entire theory. Unfortunately, almost anything can be (and has been) used to replace "A," from "commentaries on the classics" (e.g., Zeitlin, 1981) to "causal models" (e.g., Blalock, 1969). The simplicity and vagueness of our understanding of theory permits indiscriminate use of the term.

Clearly, it is time to separate different meanings of "theory," to attach different labels to these meanings, and to apply them consistently. The distinction I wish to draw here is between "theory" and "metatheory." This is, of course, not a new distinction. For example, Thomas Kuhn's (1970) discussion of "paradigms" and "puzzle-solving" is an attempt to draw a similar sort of distinction. However, the difference between the two is seldom understood clearly or presented consistently.[4] Further, there is a tendency to assume that all theory must be one or the other. Those who argue for theory see little value in metatheory; those who argue for metatheory see few possibilities for theory.

The purpose of this chapter, therefore, is to look at the distinction between theory and metatheory in more detail, to discuss the relationship be-

25

tween the two, and to suggest differences between them that affect theory assessment, choice, and growth. On the basis of this discussion I will then suggest we narrow our focus to theory for most of the remainder of the book.

ORIENTING STRATEGIES

A very large proportion of theory in sociology is in the form of metatheory. That is, it is discussion *about* theory—about what concepts should be included, about how those concepts should be linked, and about how theory should be studied. Theories of this sort provide general guidelines or strategies for approaching social phenomena and suggest the orientation the theorist should take to these phenomena; they are *orienting strategies*.

The claims of an orienting strategy are of several different kinds. First, orienting strategies make assertions about the subject matter of sociology, about the nature of social reality, and about the goals of sociological inquiry. Such statements identify what is to be treated as distinctive about sociological phenomena; they tell us what can safely be ignored in dealing with such phenomena; and they specify how one should go about dealing with the critical features that remain.

For example, in the conflict orienting strategy it is common to assert that "the history of all hitherto existing society is the history of class struggles" (Marx, 1977). This statement is often treated as a matter of contingent fact. Presumably, one can test whether or not history is rife with class conflict. However, as Turner (1982: 192) points out, such a claim can be supported only if we "define conflict so broadly that virtually any social relationship will reveal conflict." So broad a definition renders the claim empirically untestable.

The untestability of the claim does not render it useless. Rather, it merely demonstrates its strategic character, for such a statement does serve several metatheoretical purposes. It suggests that class struggles should be regarded as an inherent feature of social reality, that these struggles should be regarded as important in explaining social phenomena, and that therefore such struggles constitute an important part of the subject matter of sociology. In short, the statement indicates that class struggle is an important phenomenon that sociologists cannot afford to ignore if they wish to understand "the history of all hitherto existing societies."

Orienting strategies also provide conceptual schemes and definitions considered important and useful in describing and explaining social phenomena. They tell us what terms we are to use in describing social reality as well as *how* we are to use them. Perhaps the most obvious example of this feature appears in the functional strategy. The A-G-I-L scheme (see Parsons and Bales, 1953) identifies four survival problems, or requisites, that are to be included in any analysis of the functional character of a social system. That is, all analyses of social systems should include specifications of social structures that meet the system needs of adaptation, goal attainment, integration, and management of latent problems. These four system requisites constitute a major part of the conceptual scheme of the functional orienting strategy.

Again, conceptual schemes and definitions are often considered matters of contingent fact. Again, such treatment is inappropriate. A conceptual scheme is neither true nor false; its value is determined by its systematic import (how it functions in a body of theoretical statements) and its definitional adequacy, not by empirical support.[5] We can, for example, consider the coherence of the A-G-I-L scheme; we cannot evaluate whether adaptation, for example, is or is not empirically "true." Further, definitions are analytically true; they are tautologies. To say that goal attainment involves establishing priorities among system goals and mobilizing resources to attain them is not empirically evaluable in any way. It is true "by definition."

Finally, orienting strategies incorporate guidelines for the use of concepts and assertions in constructing and evaluating theories. These guidelines are used in identifying theoretical problems worthy of solution, in constructing reasonable solutions to those problems, and in evaluating the solutions proposed. The exchange orienting strategy provides a useful example of this property. At least in the form proposed by Homans (1974), exchange is an explicitly reductionist strategy. That is, reasonable solutions to sociological problems are to be constructed that are based on exclusively psychological principles. Attempted solutions are considered successful to the extent that they can be strictly derived from psychological principles.

As with the other major features of orienting strategies, these guidelines are generally nonempirical. One does not demonstrate the empirical truth or falsity of a reductionist strategy; one *employs* a reductionist strategy to demonstrate the truth or falsity of other ideas.

Of course, not all of these claims will be equally explicit in any particular orienting strategy. Nor will the claims be equally detailed. In fact, in a "new" strategy some types of claims may be missing altogether. However, independent of the degree of detail or explicitness or completeness of the claims of an orienting strategy, there is a special logical and empirical character that most of these claims have in common. Specifically, most of the statements of a strategy are *directives*. They are statements about values, not statements about facts. They tell us how we ought to study the social world, not what is true or false about that world. As I have demonstrated, such prescriptive arguments are largely nonempirical. Conflicts between them are generally unresolvable by either fact or reason. Put most directly, the claims of an orienting strategy generally cannot be validated as either true or false; instead, they are accepted or rejected a priori without recourse to conclusive empirical or logical evidence.

Let us look at one example of an orienting strategy—functionalism—in a little more detail. First, in the functional strategy there are a number of assertions about the subject matter of sociology and the like. These include statements indicating that the social system is the appropriate subject matter for sociology, that these systems should be viewed as having parts that perform various essential functions, and that performance of these functions maintains equilibrium in the system.[6]

Second, the conceptual and definitional scheme of functionalism includes far more than the A-G-I-L scheme. Most important, of course, is the concept of "function" itself, generally defined as a mechanism for maintaining a social unit. Functions may be identified as "manifest" (consciously motivated) or "latent" (not so motivated). Some functions are "requisite" (essential to the survival of the unit). There may even be "functional equivalents" (patterns of social behavior that fulfill the same function). These and other concepts are all seen as valuable in accounting for the character of the social systems asserted as basic subject matter of sociology.

Consider, finally, some of the directives for theory construction and evaluation in the functional strategy. Perhaps the most basic of these directives is the identification of a single general theory of society as the ultimate purpose of theory construction.[7] In constructing a functional theory, one should first assume that some universal condition (e.g., the need to distribute people to social positions) is associated with properties of the social system (e.g., survival or stability); failure to fulfill the universal condition should result in the disappearance of the associated system properties. Thus, a social system that fails to distribute people to social positions cannot survive. Further, one should assume that over time particular social structures (e.g., a stratification system) develop characteristics (e.g., inequality in reward distribution) that ensure fulfillment of the universal condition.

The basic theoretical tasks for a functionalist, therefore, are to identify universal conditions, to attempt to relate these conditions to properties of the social system, and to identify social structures with specific characteristics appropriate for fulfilling the universal conditions. The result is an explanation for the existence of system properties on the basis of the presence of the appropriate social structures.

As I have suggested, all of these claims of the functionalist strategy are directive in nature. They argue for the value of functions as explanatory tools. They do not, however, provide factual information about the specific function a particular social structure fulfills. The claims of the strategy direct us to look for such functions, but do not tell us what they are. Most important, claims of this sort are unresolvable. There is no test, logical or empirical, by which one can determine that society should or should not be viewed as a system of interrelated parts with functions.

Of course, functionalism is not the only orienting strategy currently in use in sociology. Other examples include human ecology, conflict, behaviorism, interactionism, phenomenology, and ethnomethodology. In fact, most of the "theories" commonly discussed in textbooks on sociological theory are better described as orienting strategies.[8] A theorist may adopt elements of more than one strategy at a time, as, for example, in the case of Denzin's (1969) attempt to link elements of symbolic interactionism and ethnomethodology in a single strategy. In addition, theorists may invent new strategies from time to time, as in Garfinkel's (1967) development of ethnomethodology.

Orienting strategies are much like Thomas Kuhn's "paradigms," particularly in the "disciplinary matrix" sense of the term. Strategies provide the ontological and epistemological frameworks within which theory and research is performed, just as do Kuhn's paradigms. Strategies embody the scientific values of a community of scholars, just as do paradigms.

Perhaps most important, some features of the assessment, choice, and growth of strategies are similar to those of paradigms. Generally, strategies and paradigms are not assessed but assumed. To the extent that they are assessed, the assessment is largely on sociology of knowledge grounds; for example, is the strategy consistent with the cultural framework within which it arose? The choice of a strategy is basically a nonrational process, in part because of the directive character of such metatheoretical arguments. To the extent that the process is rationalized, it depends again on external grounds; for example, are there institutional resources available to support the kind of theory and research demanded by the strategy or paradigm? Finally, the growth of both strategies and paradigms is slow and noncumulative. Most metatheoretical debates are unresolvable; even when they are resolvable, that accomplishment requires a considerable amount of time. In any case, since not all such debates can be resolved, the replacement of one strategy or paradigm with another is more adequately described simply as change, not as progress or growth. To the extent that growth does occur, it is associated generally with growth of the cultural and institutional frameworks supporting the strategy or paradigm, not with the growth of theoretical knowledge itself.[9]

However, as my earlier comments suggest, there are some important differences between strategies and paradigms. One is that orienting strategies need not reign imperially over an entire discipline as Kuhn sometimes suggested paradigms should. Several different orienting strategies may attract adherents at one time, which is not the case with paradigms. Even if one strategy is dominant during a particular historical period (as some argued was the case with functionalism in the 1950s), other strategies are likely to maintain some level of support (as did conflict and interactionism in the 1950s). Furthermore, orienting strategies need not be as incommensurable as Kuhn required paradigms to be. Although I do not wish to underestimate the difficulty of relating one strategy to another, they can sometimes be related and compared in at least a limited fashion. Denzin's paper is the best illustration of this (and the somewhat indignant response by Zimmerman and Wieder [1970] shows the difficulty inherent in such integrative attempts).

To review, orienting strategies are relatively coherent bodies of metatheoretical statements, including

(1) assertions about
     (a) the subject matter of sociology,
     (b) the nature of social reality, and
     (c) the goals of sociological inquiry;

(2) conceptual schemes and definitions considered important in analyzing social phenomena; and

(3) guidelines for the use of concepts and assertions in
     (a) selecting theoretical problems,
     (b) devising solutions to those problems, and
     (c) evaluating the solutions.

The claims of an orienting strategy are directive, rather than factual. Consequently, conflicting claims of different strategies are not generally resolvable by recourse to logic or empirical observation. In short, orienting strategies are not theories but metatheories.

UNIT THEORIES

A somewhat smaller, but still significant, proportion of theory in sociology is concerned with the presentation and evaluation of theoretical statements, rather than with the determination of which statements *should* be presented and evaluated. These statements, whether they are called "propositions," "axioms," "causal models," or whatever, are intended as explanations of particular abstract sociological problems. Thus, we may have individual or *unit theories* dealing separately with a wide variety of sociological phenomena—from Durkheim's (1951) explanation of egoistic suicide to Lenski's (1954) theory of status crystallization.

Unit theories are sometimes stated formally, sometimes discursively. In either case, the basic structure of a unit theory includes a set of concepts and a set of theoretical assertions relating those concepts to each other in an account of some sociological phenomenon. Sometimes the structure of a unit theory also includes definitions of some of the concepts and a specification of the scope of application of the theory; frequently, however, these elements are left implicit.

The statements in a unit theory have a logical and empirical character different from the statements in an orienting strategy. The assertions in a unit theory are empirically testable, either directly or indirectly; conflicts between them are frequently resolvable through appeal to fact or reason. Basically, while orienting strategies prescribe *how* to construct and evaluate unit theories, unit theories *are* the particular theoretical constructions that are to be evaluated.

Again let us turn to an example to illustrate these points. Merton's (1938) account of social structure and anomie includes at least three basic kinds of concepts: societally defined goals, legitimized means for achieving those goals, and a variety of types of deviant (i.e., anomic) behavior. The most important theoretical statement in Merton's theory asserts that structural inconsistency between societally defined goals and opportunities to use legitimized means to achieve those goals leads to deviance.

No explicit definitions are provided for "societal goals" or for "legitimized means." The various types of deviance, however, are explicitly defined in terms of the particular kind of inconsistency between goals and opportunity structure involved. If the goals and means are both available, no deviance occurs; the actor "conforms" (accepts both goals and means). If the goals are available but not the means, the actor "innovates" (accepts the goals and rejects the means). If the means are available, but not the goals, the actor "ritualizes" (accepts the means and rejects the goals). If neither the means nor the goals are available, the actor "retreats" (rejects both means and goals). If the actor substitutes (accepts) new goals and means for the socially defined and legitimated ones, he or she "rebels."

Finally, no explicit statement of scope is provided. That is, no boundaries are placed on the application of the theory; it is implicitly assumed to account for all forms of deviant behavior.[10]

Merton's account clearly has the logical and empirical character of a unit theory. Suppose, for example, that both societally defined goals and legitimized means for achieving those goals are available to a particular actor. Under those circumstances, Merton argues, the actor will conform; he or she will accept those means and goals. If the actor instead innovates— rejects the legitimized means—the theory is falsified. Certainly, then, at least some portions of Merton's argument are testable.[11]

Unit theories are somewhat similar to Kuhn's "puzzle solutions." Both result from the application of a particular metatheoretical framework. Both focus on very specific, relatively narrow empirical issues. Resolution of those issues depends very heavily on empirical grounds. And in both cases negative resolutions (i.e., failures to support the unit theory or the puzzle solution empirically) do not generally impinge directly on the status of the metatheoretical framework.

Once again, however, there are some important differences. In particular, unit theories need not be associated with a dominant orienting strategy, whereas the puzzle-solving activity of "normal science" depends on its association with an overarching paradigm. In fact, valuable unit theories are often developed *before* their metatheoretical underpinnings are even made explicit. Orienting structures may emerge (and become dominant) as a result of the success of their unit theories. In contrast, puzzle-solving cannot occur without the prior establishment of a paradigm. Furthermore, the failure of a unit theory empirically reflects on the value of theory at least as much as it does on the theorist; the failure to solve an empirical puzzle in normal science reflects only on the ingenuity of the theorist under most circumstances.

To summarize, unit theories are bodies of statements about sociological phenomena. At a minimum, they include

(1)   a set of concepts (either explicitly or implicitly defined),

(2)   a set of assertions relating these concepts to each other in an account of a sociological problem, and

(3)   a specification of the scope of application of the assertions (although this is usually only implicit).

The authors of almost all of the theory construction texts I cited in Chapter 1 had unit theories in mind when they presented their ideas. In fact, when most sociologists think about the properties they assume a good theory should have (e.g., testability, precision), they are invariably thinking in terms of unit theories. Unfortunately, when most sociologists think of examples of theories (e.g., exchange "theory," conflict "theory"), they are invariably thinking in terms of orienting strategies.[12]

THE RELATIONSHIP BETWEEN
ORIENTING STRATEGIES AND UNIT THEORIES

Although the distinction between theory and metatheory, between unit theories and orienting strategies, is a basic and important one, there is still quite a bit of confusion about it. Probably because of this confusion, a great many sociologists, having made the distinction, proceed to ignore it. Those who do not ignore it tend to assume that only one of these kinds of theory is useful; the other kind is either imperfect or useless. As a result, sociologists (including theorists) tend to evaluate all "theory" on criteria appropriate only to one kind.

Consider, for example, the "general propositions" in the 1974 edition of Homans's *Social Behavior: Its Elementary Forms*. These propositions are considered by many to be tautological. To cite only one instance, the first proposition posits a relationship between reward and performance. Reward is later defined in terms of performance. Consequently, the proposition posits only a relationship between a concept and itself; it is tautological. From the point of view of most theorists, tautologies are to be avoided since they are inherently untestable. Homans's propositions must therefore be considered seriously flawed.

I would argue however that this evaluation involves a misapplication of criteria, based on a misconception of the true character of Homans's argument. Suppose we treat the entire argument as metatheory. Under these circumstances, the relationship between reward and performance may be viewed as definitional: "Reward" means "that for which one will perform." As a metatheoretical statement, this definition directs us to (1) consider rewards important in explaining social behavior and (2) identify rewards by whether or not behavior (performance) is elicited by them. These are certainly reasonable metatheoretical directives for a behavioral orienting strategy. Thus, when metatheoretical criteria are applied, the tautologies in Homans's propositions constitute a virtue, not a flaw.

This is in fact the way most behaviorists (including Homans) treat the propositions in their work. The relationship between reward and performance is not tested but assumed. Instead, what is tested is the relationship between reward and something else (say, bargaining tactics) in behavioral terms. Nevertheless. most work in behaviorism continues to label Homans's propositions as "theory." The only consistent exception to this seems to be the work of Richard Emerson.[13]

The ethnomethodology orienting strategy provides another instance of the misapplication of theoretical criteria. Specifically, ethnomethodologists argue that the appropriate focus of sociological investigation is the study of methods actors use to achieve a sense of reality. However, theory begins by assuming some vision of reality. From a metatheoretical point of view, then, theory ought to be avoided, since it is "unquestioning."

Again, I argue that this is a misapplication of evaluative criteria, based on a misconception of theory. To require theory to question its own grounds of reality is to make it metatheory, not better theory. Furthermore, one cannot test anything without assuming some ground of reality. Hence, as a metatheoretical directive, the ethnomethodological focus on methods for achieving a sense of reality is perfectly reasonable; it is simply a call for theories with a particular kind of substantive focus. However, as a call for the abolition of theories because they are not metatheories, it is worthless.

Why are such problems of misapplication or misidentification so common? As I have suggested, some are either unaware of or are confused by the distinction between theory and metatheory. Others, I suspect, simply choose to treat their own brand of theory as imperial. Thus, for metatheoretically oriented sociologists, theory is simply "narrow formalism," while for theoretically oriented sociologists, metatheory is "empty metaphysics."

In fact, both kinds of theory are necessary. To theorize at all, one *must* assume some kind of metatheoretical framework. That framework specifies what problems are worth investigating, what tools are useful in constructing theories, and what solutions are legitimate to consider. But none of this actually solves any sociological problem. One must still choose a problem, apply the appropriate tools to the construction of a theory, and evaluate the solution that theory provides. In effect, then, theory *is* "narrow formalism" without metatheory; metatheory *is* "empty metaphysics" without theory.

Thus, although theory and metatheory are quite distinct, they are very closely related. Put most directly, the generation, analysis, and evaluation of a unit theory requires the adoption of an orienting strategy. Similarly, the implementation of an orienting strategy requires the generation, analysis, and evaluation of a unit theory.

LIMITING OUR FOCUS

Theory assessment, choice, and growth arise as issues whether we are talking about orienting strategies or unit theories. However, the processes involved in dealing with those issues are not the same. Perhaps the most important difference is in the relevance of empirical observation to the claims made. As we have seen, empirical observation is directly relevant to the claims of a unit theory; it is largely irrelevant to the claims of an orienting strategy, since many of those claims are either untestable empirically or unresolvable logically by their very nature.

In the remaining chapters we will focus on assessment, choice, and growth with respect to unit theories.[14] This does not imply that the assessment, choice, and growth of orienting strategies is unimportant or uninteresting. On the contrary, it is a fascinating subject in its own right and, for that reason, would require another book.[15]

Nor does this limitation in focus imply that the assessment, choice, and growth of unit theories are unaffected by the strategies with which the theories are associated. However, it seems wiser to consider first the various forms that theory assessment, choice, and growth may take and then to consider how metatheoretical issues may affect those processes. To discuss the influence of metatheory on processes we have not yet identified would merely confuse the issues.

Thus, although I shall have a few comments to make about orienting strategies in the next three chapters, for the most part the issue of metatheoretical impact on the assessment, choice, and growth of theory shall be deferred for consideration until Chapter 6.

Chapter 3

Theoretical Context

THE PROBLEM

In Chapter 1 I argued that differences in theoretical context have a significant impact on the assessment, choice, and growth of theories. That claim is actually a fairly complex one, involving at least three subsidiary claims:

(1) There are different theoretical contexts, different ways in which theories may be related to each other.

(2) The nature of theory assessment and choice change as a function of the type of relation between theories.

(3) Different types of relations between theories represent different patterns of theory growth or development.

My purpose in this chapter and the next is to elaborate and justify these claims. In particular, in this chapter I identify, describe, and illustrate a number of different ways in which theories appear to be related to each other. In the following chapter I consider the nature of the assessment and choice situations associated with each of these types of relations and discuss the pattern of theory development each relation represents. Chapter 4 then concludes with some suggestions for guiding theory development.

TYPES OF THEORETICAL RELATIONS

What does it mean to say that two or more theories are "related" to each other? More specifically, what feature or features must those theories have in common if we are to consider them related? There are several possibilities. For example, theories may be said to be related because they share a problem focus or a base of relevent obervations; that is, the predictions of the theories may apply in similar empirical circumstances. This is the sort of "relationship" the theories in Stinchcombe's analysis manifest. However, as we have seen, theoretical relations based entirely on empirical similarities do not adequately capture the variety of assessment and choice circumstances that may arise.

Theories might also be described as related because they share methods of observation and inference (e.g., participant observation or regression analysis). Yet, here too, the basis of the relationship seems to be entirely empirical, and therefore likely to be inadequate for the task.

What then *does* it mean to describe theories as related? Basically, we think of theories as being related when they share some structural elements: concepts, definitions, propositions, derivations, or scope conditions. The modifications made in theories invariably involve changes in one or more of these elements. We ought therefore to be able to describe different types of theoretical relations in terms of differences in the degree to which they share these structural elements and in the kinds of elements they share.

We will consider several of the more basic types of theoretical relations in the sections that follow. Each relation will be described in terms of the degree of similarity in (1) structure, (2) problem focus, and (3) character of predictions for the theories involved in the relation. For each type of relation several examples will be identified and discussed to help demonstrate the general applicability of the typology.

Although this typology of theoretical relations is intended to be basic and to be as representative as possible, it is probably not exhaustive. If for no other reason than that each type is described in idealized terms, there are bound to be a number of instances that do not fit. Nevertheless, the typology should be sufficient to allow me to demonstrate the points to be made in Chapter 4.

Four of the relations to be discussed are based primarily on some form of structural similarity. The fifth is based primarily on similarity in problem focus. What I hope to show in Chapter 4 is that the relations based on structural similarity seem likely to be much more important in analyzing theory growth and development than the relation based on similarity in problem focus.

Elaboration

Sometimes a new theory is used to make an older theory more general or specific. The new theory T(2) has a theoretical structure very similar to that of its predecessor T(1). It addresses a similar sociological problem or is applied to a similar data base of empirical observations. However, T(2) is in some sense more comprehensive, more precise, more rigorous, or has greater empirical support than T(1), from which it was generated. Thus, the predictions of T(2) "say more" (i.e., they are more comprehensive or precise) or "fit better" (i.e., they are better-supported empirically) than the predictions of T(1). Within their common explanatory domain the predictions of T(1) and T(2) either conflict over only a small part of that domain or do not conflict at all.

This sort of relation is *elaboration*. Its properties are summarized in the diagrams in Figure 1. The first diagram represents the degree to which the theories share structural elements. The second diagram represents the degree to which the theories share problem foci. The third diagram represents the degree to which predictions of the theories conflict within the area of common problem focus.

In the area of stratification Stinchcombe (1963) is clearly an elaboration of Davis and Moore (1945). Both theories address the same sociological issue: How is it that rewards come to be distributed unequally among positions in society? Both assume that the answer is functional in character. Some positions are considered more important than others because they uniquely perform a necessary function in society. If the skills needed for these positions are scarce, society attaches differential rewards to the positions to ensure that appropriately talented people fill the most important positions.[16] Consequently, given a particular level of scarcity of relevant skills, the greater the functional importance of a position, the greater the rewards that accrue to it. Similarly, at a given level of functional importance of positions, the greater the scarcity of relevant skills, the greater the rewards that accrue to the position.

Davis and Moore make predictions only at this most general level. Stinchcombe suggests this may be one of the reasons for the paucity of research on Davis and Moore's theory. Therefore, he makes several more specific predictions, proposed as testable empirical consequences of the theory. For example, during wartime, the rewards accruing to the military should increase relative to others, since their role has become functionally more important. Similarly, the degree of reward inequality *within* the military should also increase, since the talents needed in the upper echelons are scarce.

This example involves elaboration through increasing empirical specification. The two theories have the same underlying theoretical structure and address the same issue. However, Stinchcombe makes more specific, more testable predictions that do Davis and Moore.

Elaboration also occurs in the area of equity theory and distributive justice. Specifically, Adams (1965) may be considered an elaboration of

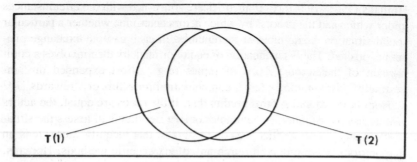

Theoretical Structure

Theories T(1) and T(2) share large parts of their theoretical structures.

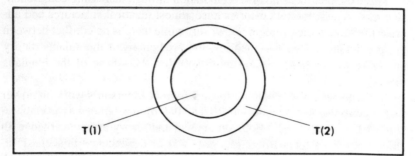

Domain of Explanation

The phenomena explained by theory T(1) are a subset of those explained by T(2).

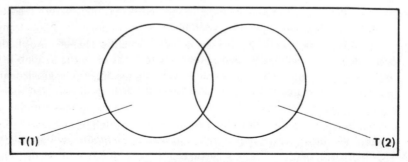

Conflict in Predictions

The predictions of theories T(1) and T(2) do not conflict or conflict only over a very small part of their common explanatory domain.

Figure 1: Elaboration

Homans (1961 [1974]). Both theories are concerned with the circumstances under which and the process by which actors determine whether a particular social situation is equitable or inequitable. In each case an exchange process is posited. The determination of equity or inequity then involves a comparison of the actors' ratios of inputs (e.g., effort expended or "investments") to outcomes (c.g., compensation for effort or "rewards").[17]

Both Homans and Adams predict that, if the ratios are equal, the actors will assess the situation as equitable; otherwise, they will assess the situation as inequitable. Adams goes on to suggest that inequity causes tension that actors seek to reduce through any of six specific methods. Homans, however, does not systematically consider actors' reactions to inequitable situations.

This example, then, involves elaboration through increasing comprehensiveness. Again, the two theories have almost identical structures and address the same basic problem. However, while there is no conflict between the predictions of the two theories, the predictions of the Adams theory are more comprehensive (and more specific) than those of the Homans theory.

Still another form of elaboration arises from Emerson's work on power and dependence. Here, Emerson (1972a, 1972b) may be seen as an elaboration of Emerson (1962). Both versions of the theory are concerned with the process by which differences in power or dependence in social relationships come to be equalized or "balanced." The basic structure of both theories is the same. First, power is defined in terms of dependence on others for rewards, with the amount of dependence on others a function of (1) the value to the actors of the rewards they seek and (2) the availability of alternative sources of those rewards to the actors. Second, actors tend to balance their relative dependence on one another. Finally, four balancing "operations" are specified, corresponding to whether changes are made in the values of one's own or of the other's rewards or in the availability of alternative sources of reward to one's self or to the other. The later formulation simply states these ideas more formally and rigorously than does the earlier theory.

Both formulations predict that balanced situations will be stable and that unbalanced situations move toward balance (or are cognitively distorted). The 1962 formulation simply indicates that these things will occur. The 1972 formulation, by contrast, specifies how they occur in operant psychological terms. In addition, the later theory makes predictions about power/dependence behavior in networks of more than two actors; the earlier formulation dealt only with situations involving two actors.

Thus, Emerson's work involves elaboration through formalization and through increasing scope. The theoretical structures and the problem foci of the two theories are virtually identical. However, the predictions of the 1972 formulation are much more rigorously derived and are expanded to cover situations involving more than two actors; no conflict between predictions of the two formulations arises.

Other examples of elaboration abound. For example, in deviance, the formalization and empirical specification of Sutherland's (1937) principles of differential association in DeFleur and Quinney (1966) is a form of elaboration. So too is the extension and refinement of Thibaut and Kelley's (1959) exchange principles of interdependence in interpersonal relations in Kelley and Thibaut (1978). In mobility theory the general framework developed by Mayer (1972) is an elaboration of the "mover/stayer" model proposed by Blumen et al. (1955) and Prais (1955). Dahrendorf's (1959) account of class conflict through imperatively coordinated associations is in many ways an elaboration of Marx's earlier account (e.g., Marx, 1848 [1977]). Merton's (1938) discussion of anomie is an elaboration of Durkheim (1897 [1951]). Coser's (1956) analysis of the functions of social conflict is largely an elaboration of Simmel (1908 [1955]).

Elaboration is the type of relation most sociologists think of as growth or development. Certainly, it is a common relation in sociology, particularly when the elaboration is primarily empirical in nature (i.e., when each new theory is designed to fit an established data base more closely). More direct theoretical elaborations (e.g., formalizations, changes in scope or precision) are perhaps somewhat less common.

Variation

In some situations the structure of a theory reveals slightly different ways in which the theory's account may be specified. Under these circumstances the original theory is likely to generate a new theory that incorporates one of these slightly different conceptualizations. Ordinarily the theoretical structure and the focus of explanation of the new theory T(2) are almost identical to those of the earlier theory T(1). The theories differ only in that they incorporate slightly different working mechanisms. Consequently, they differ only on a very limited set of grounds in such a way that the theories make directly conflicting predictions in that limited area. However, unlike elaboration, neither theory initially "says more" or "fits better" than the other; the predctions of both are usually equally comprehensive or equally supported by previous data.

This type of relation is *variation*. Its critical features are summarized in Figure 2. Variation is represented in the work of Cohen (1955) and Cloward and Ohlin (1960) on delinquent subcultures. Both theories attempt to account for the presumed concentration of deviance in lower socioeconomic classes. Both draw heavily on Merton's earlier (1938) analysis of social structure and anomie. Inconsistencies between societal goals and the availability of legitimate means of achieving these goals create "strains," which are manifested in a variety of forms of deviance. Both emphasize the importance of deviant subcultures in explaining the character and location of this deviance.

However, the explanatory mechanisms used by Cohen and by Cloward and Ohlin differ somewhat. For Cohen, delinquent behavior results from status frustration. That is, status is the societal goal that working class youths have few opportunities to achieve. The resulting strain encourages these youths to join delinquent subcultures, which provide different status goals they can achieve. In contrast, for Cloward and Ohlin wealth is the societal goal that working class youths are generally prevented from achieving. The resulting strain again encourages the youths to join delinquent subcultures. However, in this case different goals are not substituted; instead, the accumulation of wealth is stressed even more, to the point at which the use of illegitimate (e.g., criminal) means of achieving the goal is required. Hence, for Cohen, subcultural deviance is largely nonutilitarian in character; for Cloward and Ohlin, on the other hand, subcultural deviance is primarily utilitarian.

Finally, these differences in explanatory mechanism lead to some differences in predictions. For example, Cohen suggests that delinquent youths go through a process of reaction formation against the dominant values of society, thereby enabling them to adapt better to the values of the deviant subculture. No such process is predicted by Cloward and Ohlin.

Thus we have variation. Two theories share the same basic structure and have the same problem focus. However, they propose slightly different explanatory mechanisms in dealng with that problem and, as a result, make slightly different predictions over a very limited part of their common explanatory domain.

Variation is also represented in the work of Holland and Leinhardt (1971) and Hallinan (1974) on networks of positive sentiment. Both theories are concerned with the degree of transitivity of social relations. Generalizing from the assumptions of theories of cognitive balance, each develops an exhaustive listing of the combinations of relations of positive sentiment that may exist in triads of actors. Some of these combinations are classified as

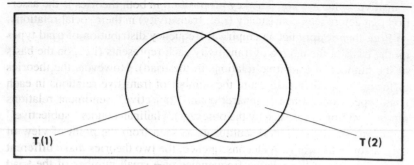

Theoretical Structure

Theories T(1) and T(2) share large parts of their theoretical structures.

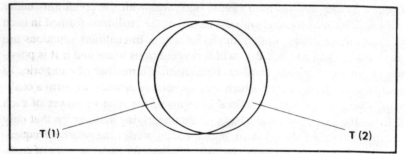

Domain of Explanation

The phenomena explained by theories T(1) and T(2) are virtually identical.

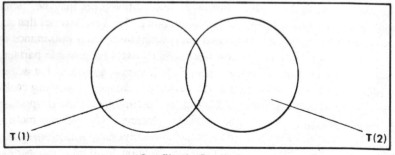

Conflict in Predictions

The predictions of theories T(1) and T(2) conflict only over a very limited part of their common domain.

Figure 2: Variation

transitive; some are not. The key proposition in both theories is the assertion that actors seek consistency (i.e., transitivity) in their social relations.

Both theories predict an empirical frequency distribution of triad types on the basis of the degree of transitivity each represents (i.e., on the basis of the number of transitive relations in the triad). However, the theories differ on how one should count the number of transitive relations in each triad type. Holland and Leinhardt count "objective" sentiment relations (actors' sentiments as seen by the observer); Hallinan counts "subjective" sentiment relations (actors' sentiments as seen from the point of view of each actor in the triad). As a consequence, the two theories make different predictions about the relative frequencies of a small number of the triad types.

Work on coalition formation also represents an example of variation. Caplow (1956) and Gamson (1961) both deal with the conditions under which coalitions form and with the nature of the coalitions formed in each kind of circumstance. Both assume that actors in coalition situations are motivated to win and that they will form coalitions when and if it is possible to win by doing so. Further, both identify a number of categories of coalition situations, within which various pairs of actors may form a coalition. These categories are defined in terms of the relative power of each actor in the situation. On the basis of the underlying assumption that only winning coalitions should form, both theories predict the relative frequency of coalitions between particular pairs of actors for each category of coalition situation.

The difference between the two theories stems from the specification of different mechanisms for the prediction of relative frequencies of coalition pairs in categories where two or more coalition pairs may be "winning" combinations. Caplow's "minimum power" theory assumes that actors in such situations are motivated also to maximize their dominance in the coalition; they will prefer coalitions with the weakest possible partner. Gamson's "minimum resource" theory, by contrast, assumes that actors in such situations are motivated also to seek the "cheapest" winning coalition; they will prefer coalitions that provide them the greatest proportion of the winnings generated by the coalition.[18] Interestingly, the two mechanisms lead to different predicted frequencies in only one coalition category, referred to as the "revolutionary" coalition situation. In all other categories, the predicted frequencies are the same. Once again, therefore, we see two very similar theories with the same problem focus and with a conflict in predictions over a very limited area.

Other examples of variation include the relation in attribution theory between Jones and Davis's (1965) theory of correspondent inferences and Kelley's (1971) theory of external attribution, as well as the relation between Deutsch and Krauss's (1962) "conflict spiral" approach and Tedeschi et al.'s (1972) "deterrence" approach to issues of bargaining and negotiation. A second example in the study of deviance is the relationship between the differential association theory of Burgess and Akers (1966) and the control theory of Hirschi (1969).

Variation is a relatively common relation. However, it is often difficult to see from the point of view of "outsiders" (i.e., those not intimately familiar with the theories involved). Often much of the structure of T(2) is left implicit since it is so similar to T(1). Further, the changes in structure are often quite subtle. Those not thoroughly familiar with the theories may frequently fail to see any important distinctions between them. The grounds of difference, at least to the outsider, may simply be too small to be noticed.

Variation is a type of relation frequently considered in the philosophy of science, perhaps because it is the only type in which the area of difference is sufficiently small that "crucial experiments" may be created. However, the outcomes of such experiments are seldom as straightforward as Stinchcombe's analysis of them (see Chapter 1) suggests. Even with crucial experiments, the outcome is seldom the direct and immediate replacement of one theoretical mechanism with another; much more frequently the outcome is likely to be the specification of a set of conditions under which each mechanism applies.

Proliferation

Consider now a situation in which ideas from one theory are used to generate a new theory concerned with a new or different sociological problem or data base. Again the new theory T(2) is similar in structure to T(1). However, in this case the predictions of the two theories are generally nonoverlapping, since they apply to different explanatory domains. In a sense, here too the predictions of T(2) "say more" or "fit better" than those of T(1), but only with respect to the newly considered problem area. They have little or nothing to say about the original problem area, where the predictions of T(1) remain appropriate.

This sort of relation we will call *proliferation*. Its properties are summarized in Figure 3. Proliferation is evident in Hannan and Freeman's (1977) application of ideas from population ecology (see especially Hawley, 1950;

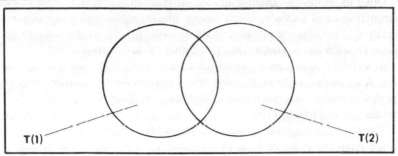

Theoretical Structure

Theories T(1) and T(2) share a limited portion of their theoretical structures.

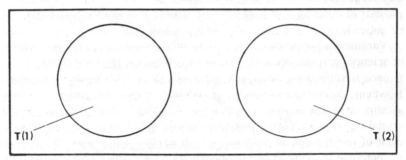

Domain of Explanation

The phenomena explained by theory T(1) are entirely different from the phenomena explained by theory T(2).

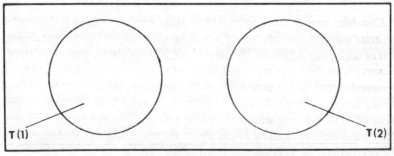

Conflict in Predictions

There is no conflict in predictions between theories T(1) and T(2).

Figure 3: Proliferation

Levins, 1968) to deal with organizational phenomena. Both are concerned with the ways in which the environment affects the structure and viability of entities within the population. Both assume that selection through competition plays an important role in mediating these effects.

However, population ecology (in particular, bioecology) is concerned more specifically with populations of biological organisms, while Hannan and Freeman are concerned with populations of social organizations. Thus, in this instance of proliferation at least, the problem foci of the proliferant theories are not even part of the same discipline. The forms of predictions in both areas are often similar to one another; for example, both may incorporate predictions about the growth of competing populations based on the same equations (the "Lotka Volterra" equations). Nevertheless, the predictions do not overlap. Nothing that bioecology has to say about the growth of populations of protozoa implies anything about the validity of the application of similar ideas to populations of *Fortune* 500 corporations.[19]

Thus, we have a clear case of proliferation. The theories have related theoretical structures but distinct problem foci and unrelated predictions.

Proliferation also describes the relation between Heider's (1944, 1946) work on cognitive organization and Newcomb's (1956) theory of interpersonal attraction. The two theories share much of their theoretical structure. Specifically, both incorporate a balance principle: Actors seek consistency in their sentiment relations with other actors. In addition, the two theories share assumptions about the consequences of the balance principle: Balance is stable, imbalance is tension-producing, and imbalance tends to be reduced.

The problem foci of the two theories are quite different, however. Heider is concerned with a *cognitive* process, with the organization of sentiments within a particular actor's mental frame of reference. Newcomb is concerned with a *communication* process, with the organization of sentiments among actors and the consequences of that organization for interpersonal attraction. Consequently, the two theories make predictions about balance that are similar in form; however, there is no overlap in those predictions, since they are applied to different phenomena at different levels of analysis.

Siegel et al.'s (1964) model and Ofshe and Ofshe's (1969) model of choice behavior also constitute a case of proliferation. Both are probability models, concerned essentially with specifying the probabilities that a particular decision will be made and that the decision made will be reciprocated. Both assume that actors are motivated by the utilities of accurate decision-making and of variability in behavior. As a result, each develops equations predicting the relative frequency of particular decisions.

But the problems of concern in the two models are radically different. Siegel et al.'s model deals with "light guessing," a completely nonsocial choice situation. Ofshe and Ofshe's model is concerned with the selection of a coalition partner, definitely a social choice situation. The predictions of the two models are therefore unrelated, despite the structural similarities; their relation is one of proliferation.

Other examples of proliferation include Miller and Dollard's (1941) extension of Hullian learning principles (first reported in Hull, 1943) to deal with learning by imitation, and Burgess and Akers's (1966) use of Skinner's (1953) principles of operant behavior in their theory of criminal behavior. Lemert's (1951) societal reaction approach to deviance is largely a proliferation from Mead's (1934) general principles regarding symbolic interaction.

As these examples may suggest, proliferation may involve several distinct subtypes. Specifically, proliferation may occur when the theorist attempts to deal with (1) the same problem at a different level of analysis, (2) a different problem at the same level of analysis, or (3) a different problem at a different level of analysis.

Proliferation suggests a sort of "branching" process in theoretical development. What is involved is an attempt to explain newly discovered phenomena or newly developed data bases—to expand theoretical ideas into new explanatory domains. Although proliferation is seldom discussed (either in sociology or in the philosophy of science) the theoretical expansiveness it represents is a critical feature of theory development. Its importance will be discussed in greater detail in Chapter 5.

Integration

In a sense, this sort of relation is the opposite of variation. Sometimes two different theories suggest very similar ways of dealing with the same sociological problem. Under these circumstances, a new theory may emerge that incorporates much of the conceptualization of both theories. In such cases at least three theories, which may or may not have similar theoretical structures, are involved. One theory T(3) consolidates many of the ideas found in T(1) and T(2) in a single formulation, usually suggesting interrelationships between those ideas. Generally speaking, predictions of T(1) and T(2) are subsumed in the structure of the new theory T(3), although it is unlikely that all will be subsumed (especially if the earlier theories are structurally unrelated). Also, the new theory ordinarily generates some additional predictions not made by either earlier theory.

This relation, labeled *integration,* is in fact a composite of other relations. That is, integrating theories may also be seen as elaborants in that

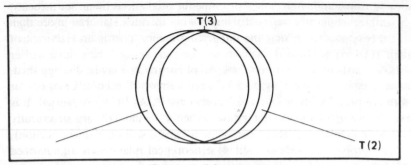

Theoretical Structure

The theoretical structure of T(3) incorporates most of the important ideas in the variant theories T(1) and T(2).

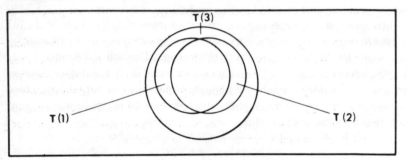

Domain of Explanation

The phenomena explained by theory T(3) include as a subset the phenomena explained by both variants T(1) and T(2).

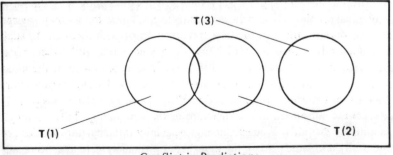

Conflict in Predictions

There is no conflict in predictions between T(3) and variants T(1) and T(2).

Figure 4: Integration of Variants

they subsume and often extend or refine the predictions of earlier theories; the difference is, of course, that integrating theories elaborate more than one theory at a time; thus the integrating theory T(3) is an elaborant of both T(1) and T(2). T(3) "says more" or "fits better" than either earlier theory. Furthermore, different subtypes of integration may be distinguished, depending on whether T(1) and T(2) are variants of each other or one or both are proliferants from an earlier theory. [20]. As I have suggested, it is even possible to consider integration when T(1) and T(2) are structurally unrelated (a relation I label "competition" and discuss in the next section).

The properties of integration as a theoretical relation are summarized in Figures 4, 5, and 6. The first figure considers the properties of integration when the integrated theories are variants. The second figure reviews the properties of integrations when the integrated theories are proliferants. The third figure presents the properties of integration when the integrated theories are unrelated (i.e., are competitors).

Bacharach and Lawler (1981) present an interesting example of the integration of variants. Their theory of bargaining subsumes most of the structure of the conflict spiral and deterrence theories (Deutsch and Krauss, 1962, and Tedeschi et al., 1972, respectively) mentioned earlier. All three theories are concerned with the relative punitive capabilities of bargaining actors and with the consequences of those capabilities for the use of tactics of threat and punishment.

Deterrence theory, represented schematically in Figure 7, makes two basic assumptions, according to Bacharach and Lawler. First, the development of punitive capabilities by either party to the interaction encourages the development of punitive capabilities by the other party. Second, the development of punitive capabilities by either party discourages the use of punitive tactics by the other.

Conflict spiral theory is shown schematically in Figure 8. In Bacharach and Lawler's account, it makes the same assumption about the mutually reinforcing effects of attempts to develop punitive capabilities and applies it to the use of threat and punitive tactics as well. That is, the development of punitive capabilities, the use of threat tactics, and the use of punitive tactics by one party *all* encourage the same actions by the other party. However, conflict spiral theory makes a very different assumption about the effect of the development of punitive capabilities on tactical moves. Specifically, it argues that the development of punitive capabilities by one party *encourages* the use of both threat and punishment tactics by that same party.

Bacharach and Lawler use the power/dependence ideas of Blau (1964) and Emerson (1962, 1972a, 1972b) to integrate these two theories. Basically,

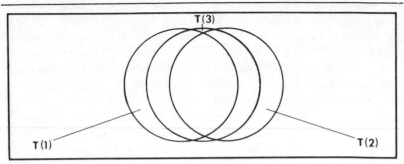

Theoretical Structure

The theoretical structure of T(3) incorporates many of the important ideas in the proliferant theories T(1) and T(2).

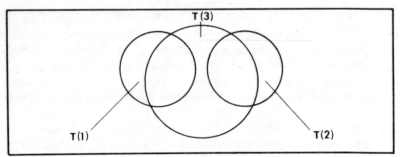

Domain of Explanation

The phenomena explained by theory T(3) include most of the phenomena explained by both proliferants T(1) and T(2).

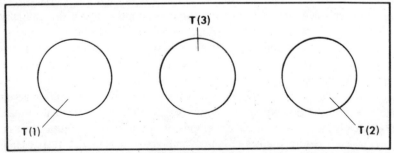

Conflict in Predictions

There is no conflict in predictions between T(3) and proliferants T(1) and T(2).

Figure 5: Integration of Proliferants

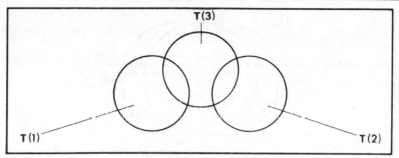

Theoretical Structure

The theoretical structure of T(3) incorporates some of the important ideas in the competing theories T(1) and T(2).

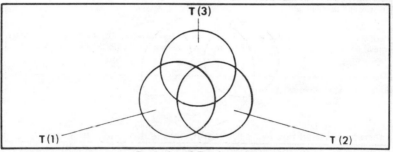

Domain of Explanation

The phenomena explained by theory T(3) include some of the phenomena explained by both competitors T(1) and T(2).

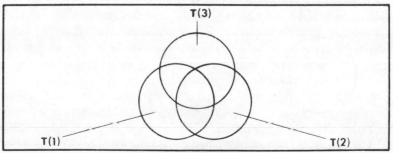

Conflict in Predictions

There is at least some conflict in predictions between T(3) and competitors T(1) and T(2).

Figure 6: Integration of Competitors

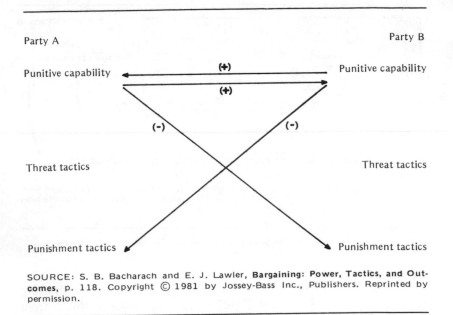

SOURCE: S. B. Bacharach and E. J. Lawler, **Bargaining: Power, Tactics, and Outcomes**, p. 118. Copyright © 1981 by Jossey-Bass Inc., Publishers. Reprinted by permission.

Figure 7: Deterrence Theory

deterrence is assumed to be applicable in situations in which the stakes in the bargaining are relatively low. As the stakes increase, the likelihood that tactics of threat and punishment will prompt counteruse increases. Once this has occurred, the conflict spiral predictions become more appropriate. Furthermore, it is impossible to return to the deterrence conditions without restructuring the bargaining situation.

Bacharach and Lawler go beyond the conditionalization of deterrence and conflict spiral theory to develop propositions concerned with the effects of the use of punitive tactics by one party on the concession behavior of the other party. Thus, their integrating theory both consolidates and extends the earlier theories of bargaining behavior.

A second, less complete example of integration appears in Cook and Emerson's (1978) work on power, equity, and commitment in exchange networks. Their theory is intended in part to integrate Emerson's earlier work on power and dependence (cited above) and ideas from equity theory (see Homans, 1961; Adams, 1965; Walster, et al., 1973). Cook and Emerson are primarily concerned with the use of power. They are concerned

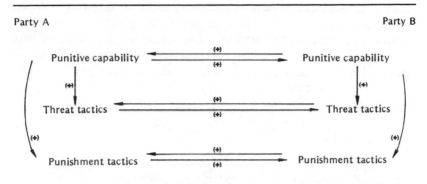

Party A   Party B

SOURCE: S. B. Bacharach and E. J. Lawler, **Bargaining: Power, Tactics, and Outcomes**, p. 126. Copyright © 1981 by Jossey-Bass Inc., Publishers. Reprinted by permission.

Figure 8: Conflict Spiral Theory

with equity only insofar as it increases dependence (thereby constraining the use of power). Further, they define equity in a manner distinct from its standard definition in equity theory. For Cook and Emerson, equity is defined as equality in the values exchanged by mutually dependent actors; for equity theorists, equity is defined as equality in the ratios of inputs to outcomes of individual actors. Thus, the integration performed by Cook and Emerson is clearly only partial.

Power/dependence theory and equity theory are probably proliferant theories, which may explain why the integration in Cook and Emerson is less complete; it is simply more difficult to consolidate theories applied to disparate areas than it is to consolidate theories applied to essentially the same area.

Given these limitations, integrating theories are a rather rare phenomenon. Even when they can be found, they often accomplish only a partial integration, as in the Cook and Emerson example. Still, integrating theories are highly desired for their parsimony, simplicity, generality, explanatory power, and other virtuous features. In fact, since integration often constitutes the "major advance" that is the clearest evidence of progress, there are frequent attempts to integrate theories that are structurally unrelated (as in Figure 6).

One instance of such an attempt is Turner's (1975, 1982) synthesis of the theories of conflict presented in Coser (1956) and in Dahrendorf (1959).

The two earlier theories share a problem focus but have little in common structurally. Coser's theory is in large part an attempt to show how a functional theory could usefully deal with conflict. Dahrendorf's theory is in large part an attempt to show how a Marxist theory could usefully deal with structural stability in society.

Turner's integration begins with a limitation in the scope of his account. Specifically, he focuses on

(1) conflict as the conscious, overt effort by parties in an interaction to thwart each other's access to scarce resources,

(2) the processes by which such conflict is created (thereby excluding concern with the consequences or functions of conflict), and

(3) differences in the severity of conflict in terms of the degree of violence involved.

Turner then posits a nine-step process through which conflict emerges. Thus, (1) in a social system of interdependent parts, (2) scarce resources may be unequally distributed. This may lead to (3) the withdrawal of legitimacy of the inequality by those disadvantaged by it. Such people are likely to become (4) initially aware of their objective interests and (5) emotionally aroused by their deprivation; (6) individual and collective outbursts of emotion and frustration may follow, leading to (7) increased intensity of conflict; (8) efforts at organization of the deprived become increasingly successful; and (9) depending on the extent and character of that organization, conflict may be more or less severe (i.e., more or less violent).

There is much in both Coser's and Dahrendorf's theories that Turner does not cover. For example, as noted above, Turner has nothing to say about the functions of conflict, which is a matter of great importance to Coser. In addition, Turner does not discuss the role of imperatively coordinated associations in conflict, a role Dahrendorf considers essential. In fact, Turner's theory is presented in different theoretical language from the two earlier theories, although it incorporates many of their ideas.

Turner also goes beyond Coser and Dahrendorf in many ways. For example, neither of the first two steps in Turner's model is considered by Coser or Dahrendorf.

Other attempts to integrate structurally unrelated theories include Denzin's (1969) attempt to integrate interactionist and ethnomethodological conceptualizations of interaction process, as well as Collins's (1975) attempt to develop a unified theory of conflict from earlier Marxist and phenomenological ideas. Unfortunately, such attempts usually fail miserably or become quite controversial. This sort of result occurs largely because both theory and metatheory are presented in the same work. It also occurs because the theories to be integrated are related only in the sense to be considered next.

Competition

In some cases a new theory is generated in an attempt to capture at least some of the explanatory domain of another theory. In these situations the theoretical structure of T(2) is essentially *dissimilar* to that of T(1). T(1) and T(2) are related theoretically only in that they have similar problem foci or similar data bases. The major differences in theoretical structure, coupled with the similarities in focus or data base, lead to relatively large areas of conflicting predictions over at least some portion of the explanatory domain of each theory. If the structure of T(2) is entirely different from that of T(1) and if the explanatory domains are identical, the predictions of the two theories could conceivably conflict at every point. Both theories may claim to "say more" or to "fit better."

The properties of this very different form of relation, *competition*, are summarized in Figure 9. The best example of competition with which I am familiar is the relation between Scheff's (1966) labeling theory and Gove's (1970) psychophysiological theory of mental illness. Both theories are concerned with specifying the conditions under which mental illness is likely to occur and with explaining the stability of deviant behavior associated with mental illness.

The two theories have virtually nothing in common structurally. Scheff considers mental illness the result of residual classification of otherwise unexplainable behavior; it is externally and socially labeled; deviant behavior stabilizes because the label becomes the basis for all interaction with the individual so labeled. Gove, however, considers mental illness the result of psychiatric or physiological disorders; it is internally generated; behavior stabilizes because such disorders are difficult to recognize and to treat.

Consequently, there are broad areas of conflict in the predictions of the two theories (e.g., with respect to the rates of voluntary commitment to mental institutions to be expected in various social situations). There is also conflict over what the predictions of each theory actually are (see, e.g., Scheff, 1974, and Gove, 1975). Overall, there is little agreement about what each theory should predict, what evidence is relevant, and how that evidence should be interpreted.

Another interesting example of competition occurs in the relation between the "power elites" and "veto groups" accounts of power in society

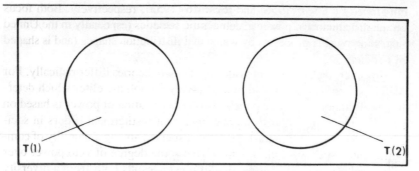

Theoretical Structure

The theoretical structures of theories T(1) and T(2) are entirely different.

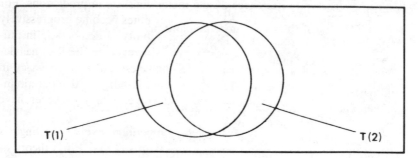

Domain of Explanation

The phenomena explained by theory T(1) and T(2) overlap to a large extent.

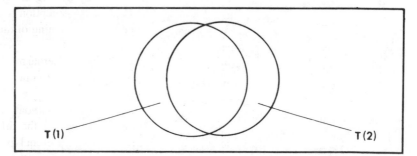

Conflict in Predictions

The predictions of theories T(1) and T(2) conflict over a very large part of their common explanatory domain.

Figure 9:   Competition

developed by Mills (1956) and Riesman (1953), respectively. Both focus on the distribution of power in democratic societies (especially in the United States) and on the processes by which that distribution shapes (and is shaped by) society.

However, the accounts provided by the two theories differ radically. For Mills, power is concentrated in a relatively monolithic elite, which determines all important public policy. This concentration of power is based on the coincidence of interests among important institutional orders in society. For Riesman, in contrast, power is dispersed among a plurality of competing interest groups, all of which have some degree of veto power over other such groups. This dispersion of power results both from a diversity of individual interests in society and from a general feeling of impotence on the part of those with power.

These structural differences dictate major conflicts in predictions. For example, Mills suggests that, because power elites become progressively unaccountable for their use of power, the stability of democratic institutions in society is progressively weakened. However, in the Riesman account, dispersion of power creates amorphousness and indeterminacy in leadership. In the short run, this *supports* the stability of democratic institutions, since no one accumulates too much power; it may, however, have deleterious effects in the long run.

A somewhat less extreme example of competition involves Festinger's (1957) theory of cognitive dissonance and Bem's (1964, 1967) theory of self-perception. Both theories attempt to explain how changes in self-perception occur. However, once again, there is little in common structurally between the two theories. For Festinger, self-perception is a cognitive process; change is a result of dissonance (inconsistency among an individual's attitudes, beliefs, and attributes). For Bem, self-perception is a behavioral process; "change" is not really change but the learning of the demand properties of new situations.

Again, differences over the predictions of the two theories generate much heat and little light. Here the differences are not so much over concrete predictions. In fact, one interpretation of Bem's argument is that it is possible to account for the same behavior outcomes as does Festinger's without incorporating his "mentalistic" assumptions. Instead, almost all the differences occur on a more basic level: Should behavior in two different types of situations (e.g., specifying one's own perceptions and inferring others' perceptions) be treated in the same way theoretically? Are there other than perceptual phenomena involved? What data are truly relevant to answering these questions?

Once again, we see a relation between theories with similar problem foci but radically different theoretical structures. The result is a predictive mess, with not only predictive discrepancies, but also disagreements over the character, relevance, and interpretation of data.

Competition is a particularly common type of theoretical relation in sociology. It occurs in stratification between Davis and Moore (1945) and critics of their functional views. It occurs in the sociology of education in the conflict between genetic and environmental accounts of the bases of intelligence. And, of course, we have already seen instances of competition in deviance, political sociology, and social psychology.

The character of competition as a theoretical relation helps to account for the high rate of failure of attempts at integration. Consider the two examples of failed integration identified in the previous section of this chapter. The Marxist and phenomenological assumptions about class conflict are neither variants nor proliferants; they are competitors. So too with the interactionist and ethnomethodological assumptions about interaction process; they constitute competing theories, not variants or proliferants. And how does one integrate theories when, because of strategy differences, the adherents cannot even agree on the grounds for dispute?

These points suggest that competition plays a radically different role in theory growth and development than do the other four relations. The character of that role will be explored in detail in the next chapter.

REVIEW

In this Chapter I have identified five different types of relations between theories. The characteristics of those types are summarized in Figure 10. Although a serious attempt has been made at being representative, the roster of types considered is probably not exhaustive; it is definitely idealized.

Nevertheless, a variety of quite basic inferences can be drawn from this typology. First, there are, in fact, several distinct types of relations that may occur between or among theories. The differences between them involve considerably more than the simple differentiation between structurally related and structurally unrelated theories (although that differentiation is, of course, quite important).

Second, the domain of explanation changes dramatically as we move from type to type. Clearly, differences in explanatory domain (i.e., problem focus or relevant data base) play an important role in defining the differences among the various types of theoretical relations.

Theoretical Structure   Domain of Explanation   Conflict in Predictions

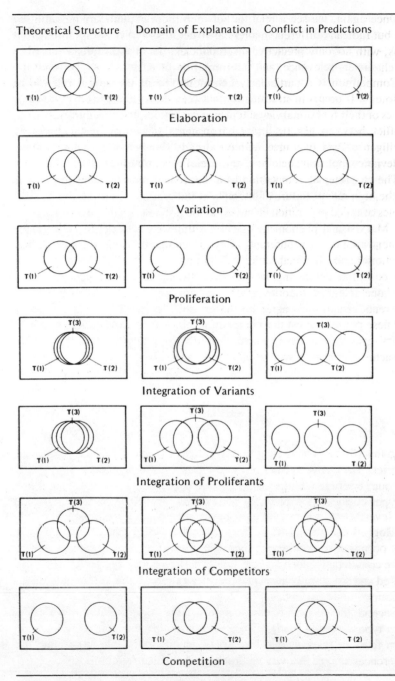

Elaboration

Variation

Proliferation

Integration of Variants

Integration of Proliferants

Integration of Competitors

Competition

Figure 10: Summary of the Types of Theoretical Relations

Third, as a consequence of the differences in explanatory domain, the character of the relation between predictions also changes as we move from type to type. Note especially that in only *two* cases do conflicting predictions arise (where data might strongly influence the choice between the theories). Further, in only one of those two cases (variation) is a choice likely to be comparatively easy to make. In the other case (competition), choice is often nearly impossible, at least on empirical grounds.

In any case, the types of theoretical relations we have discussed are clearly quite distinct. I have argued that the nature of theory assessment and choice change as a function of these types of relations, that these types therefore represent quite different kinds of theory growth or development. That is the issue to be taken up in the next chapter.

Chapter 4

Theoretical Context and Theory Growth

THE CLAIMS

As Chapter 3 has shown, there clearly are several distinct types of relations that may exist between theories. But do those distinctions make a difference? In this chapter I argue that they do. Theory assessment and theory choice are both a function of the type of theoretical relation involved; further, there are different kinds of theory growth associated with each type. In short, theory assessment and choice (and therefore also theory growth) should be seen as multidimensional processes.

A number of implications follow immediately from this characterization. The most basic and important of these implications involve (1) our understanding of the nature of theory construction and evaluation and (2) our ability to guide theoretical development.

Consider first the nature of theory construction and evaluation. If the different types of theoretical relations do in fact represent different types of assessment, choice, and growth, then, clearly, different construction tasks are involved in each type. Further, different criteria should be required for the evaluation of different types of construction efforts. The implication is that theory construction and evaluation are also seen to be multidimensional; *the nature of the task and the criteria by which the effort is evaluated change as a function of the type of relation involved.*

The multidimensionality of theory assessment, choice, and growth also suggests some guidelines for conducting theoretical activity if our goal is cumulative knowledge. Of course, no one can devise guidelines that would guarantee theoretical growth and development. However, it is possible to identify and remove some of the obstacles that stand in the way of such development. For example, not all types of relations promote development equally, largely because the theoretical issues involved in the respective construction tasks are not equally resolvable. The sensible theorist therefore would not devote an equal amount of time to the pursuit of each type of theoretical relation; the effort simply would not be fruitful.

Each of these points is considered in some detail below. The chapter concludes with some suggestions for the elaboration of a general strategy for cumulative theory development, a strategy that will be explicated more thoroughly in Chapter 5.

THE MULTIDIMENSIONALITY
OF THEORY DEVELOPMENT

The distinctions between the different types of theoretical relations, I have argued, imply several further distinctions. For each type of relation

(1)   the nature and purpose of the theory construction task is different; and

(2)   the criteria relevant to the evaluation of success at that task are also different; therefore,

(3)   the character of the assessment situation differs;

(4)   the properties of the choice situation differ; and

(5)   the kind of theory growth involved is different.

To demonstrate these claims, let us consider each of the types of relations in turn.

Elaboration

In the case of elaboration the theory construction task is to say something more about the same phenomenon (or perhaps to say it more precisely) while maintaining consistency with what was said before. The goal in performing the task is twofold: first to show how T(1) (the original theory) "fits into" T(2) (the elaborating theory); second, to suggest some ideas in T(2) that are not suggested by T(1). Thus, Emerson's (1972a, 1972b) version of power/dependence theory is intended both to formalize his 1962 account of the process (i.e., to fit the entire theory into a more rigorous operant framework) and to expand the scope of the theory to include power/dependence *networks* involving two or more actors.

Achieving the first goal depends on establishing the derivability of the principles of T(1) from the principles of T(2). Achieving the second goal depends on showing any one of a variety of different things: that T(2) is greater in scope than T(1), that it has greater rigor or greater precision, that its principles are deeper or simpler, and so on. Thus, a number of evaluative criteria are relevant to the assessment of attempts to elaborate a theory. Derivability is always involved. One or more of scope, rigor, precision, and the like are always involved. In the Emerson case, scope, rigor, and precision all seem to be involved.

Although the number of different criteria that may be involved in evaluating an elaboration is rather large, the assessment situation is a comparatively straightforward one. First, no matter how many of the criteria are involved, it is usually possible to specify just which ones they are. Perhaps because of the extensive consideration of many of these criteria in theory construction and in the philosophy of science, most sociologists are relatively clear about what they are trying to accomplish when they elaborate a theory. There is little doubt in Stinchcombe's (1963) formulation of the functional theory of stratification, for instance, that an attempt was being made to develop more specific, empirically testable propositions that could be derived from Davis and Moore's more general assumptions.

Second, seldom are all the relevant criteria involved at once. An attempt to increase the scope of a theory, for example, does not always involve an attempt to increase the precision of the theory as well. Adams (1965) increased the scope of equity theory by explicating another part of the process—actors' *reactions* to perceived inequities. He did not, however, generate a more determinate or precise account of how equity judgments are made than Homans had.

Third, applying the relevant criteria is, in general, a simple and immediate process. There is relatively high agreement, for instance, about what constitutes greater scope or precision in a theory. Further, judgments about such things often can be made reasonably quickly, simply by inspection. It does not require inordinate analytical or observational skill to determine exactly in what way and to what extent Adams's formulation increases the scope of equity theory.

All of this is *not* to say that elaboration is a nonproblematic theoretical task. Elaborations can be quite complex; some criteria (e.g., simplicity) are not easy to apply or interpret; sometimes improvement with respect to one criterion (e.g., scope) is at the expense of deterioration with respect to another (e.g., precision). Nevertheless, as we shall see below, the assessment situation for elaboration is quite clear, *relative to the assessment situations for the other types of relations.*

The choice situation presented by elaboration involves a form of replacement. That is, T(2) is intended to serve as a replacement for T(1). However, often the replacement that takes place is far from complete. Since T(1) is not really "wrong," just more limited than T(2), it may continue to be the preferred theory in many circumstances. While Emerson's 1962 theory has nowhere near the scope, rigor, or precision of his later formulation, the earlier version may still be preferred in contexts in which only a broad account of power/dependence processes in two-actor situations is needed. Thus, choosing between the two theories may depend on the purpose for which the choice is made; a choice based on simplicity or applicability may be quite different from one based on clarity or sophistication.[21]

Note that evaluations of empirical support need not be directly involved in the assessment and choice process for elaborations. Since one of the purposes of an elaboration is that it be able to "say the same things" as another theory, evaluations of empirical support will not discriminate between the two in that context. Only to the extent that an elaboration goes beyond the other theory to "say more" will empirical support be a relevant issue. Hence, empirical evaluations of Adams's equity theory are likely to focus more on what is new in that theory—the specification of particular reactions to inequity—and less on what Adams retained of Homans's ideas. Further, evaluations of empirical support may be relatively unimportant if the elaborating theory simply says things more rigorously or precisely without introducing new "things to say." The new ideas about exchange networks are what create the impetus for further empirical testing of Emerson's ideas. Without them, data supportive of the earlier theory would be equally supportive of the new theory; while testing might still occur, its evaluative importance would be lessened. Finally, as in the case of Stinchcombe's derivations from the functional theory of stratification, elaboration may be necessary before extensive empirical evaluation is even possible if the original theory makes few empirical predictions.

The kind of growth represented by elaboration is *linear*. Each new elaboration is a single theory that subsumes all (or almost all) of the content of its predecessor and adds something to that content as well. Progress is direct and cumulative in the sense in which that term is traditionaly understood. That is, elaboration involves a direct line of development of knowledge from a theory to its ever more inclusive successors.[22]

Variation

The theory construction situation presented by variation is quite different from that presented by elaboration. Here the task is to cover the same ground as another idea, using similar ideas but a different explanatory mechanism. The basic objective in developing a variant is to formulate the theory in such a way that the differences in predictions it makes can be readily evaluated.

Thus, Gamson (1961) created a theory of coalition formation virtually identical to the Caplow (1956) theory, with only one significant change in assumptions. Further, that single assumptive difference generates but one significant difference in predictions. Under such circumstances, it becomes possible to focus attention specifically on the limited area of difference. Since so many features of the theories and their predictions are held in common, any differences in result cannot be attributed to them; only the limited areas of theoretical and predictive difference can be the source of empirical difference.

Variants give the theorist two or more options as to how to proceed in further theorizing. Achieving the objective may involve either the selection of one of those options or the specification of conditions under which each option should be selected. Thus, the criteria appropriate for the evaluation of attempts at variation are those useful in making such selections. Ordinarily, this will involve the evaluation of relative empirical support. One alternative may simply provide a better account of the available data than the other alternative. Such has been the case in the study of networks of positive sentiment. Hallinan's (1974) theory provided a somewhat more satisfactory prediction for the relative frequency of a few of the types of sentiment triads than did the Holland and Leinhardt (1971) theory. The issue becomes a little more complex if both alternatives are potentially useful under some circumstances. In this case one must be able to specify and evaluate the conditions under which each alternative is expected to apply.

Performing these evaluations is often not as simple as it may appear at first glance. If the two variants are significantly different in scope, precision, or other such features, it may be very difficult to make the required comparisons. In the case of the Cohen (1955) and Cloward and Ohlin (1960) variants of strain theory, scope is not even specified, nor is either argument very precise. Thus, it becomes difficult to make any telling comparisons between them. Thus, the assessment situation is likely to be relatively clear only if these features are well-specified and virtually identical for both theories. The degree of difficulty in interpreting results increases as the degree of specificity and the degree of similarity in the theories decreases.

The choice situation represented by variation may involve either replacement or conditionalization. In either case, empirical support is the primary basis for the choice made. However, in the case of conditionalization, neither theory can be chosen on the basis of overall empirical support. Since T(1) is wrong under some circumstances and T(2) is wrong under some circumstances, the choice between T(1) and T(2) is based more on the specification of the conditions of interest than on overall empirical support. Thus, the Hallinan and Holland and Leinhardt models of positive sentiment relations may each be treated as correct, but only under different circumstances. Specifically, Hallinan's model would be better when the perspecive of each individual actor in a sentiment situation is important; Holland and Leinhardt's model would be better when an external, "objective" perspective is more appropriate. Although overall the data offer more support to Hallinan's model, the choice of Holland and Leinhardt's model cannot be ruled out.

Theory growth through variation is growth *in parallel*. In fact, variation is a form of "friendly conflict" in which the development of either theory supports the key ideas in both of them. As a result, both theories are likely to be pursued at the same time until one or the other shows itself to be more satisfactory, or until the conditions under which each is more satisfactory can be identified. Resolution of the conflict supports the basic principles of both theories, no matter how the conflict is resolved. Thus, the parallel paths of growth of variants are likely to be relatively short-lived. The theorist is usually much more strongly attached to the basic principles of a theory than to a specific mechanism for implementing them. If the mechanism is not well supported, he or she is likely to sacrifice it relatively quickly.

Proliferation

With proliferation the theory construction task is to apply to a new domain the concepts and themes developed in an already established theory. In performing this task the theorist is attempting to "establish a beachhead" in attacking a new problem, to link the accounts of previously disparate phenomena. Newcomb (1956) sought to apply notions of cognitive balance to the phenomenon of interpersonal attraction. Ofshe and Ofshe (1969) sought to account for the process of partner choice in multiperson coalition situations using a probability model based on "light guessing." Hannan and Freeman (1977) sought to apply notions of population ecology to organizational phenomena.

The motivation may be internal to the theory, in the sense that proliferation of the theory is intended to show its range of applicability. Newcomb's proliferation seems to involve this motivation to a large extent. Balance ideas are at the core of concern; attraction is simply another area to which those ideas may be applied. However, the motivation may also be external, in the sense that proliferation is needed to help make sense of a new area. This motivation seems to underlie the Ofshe and Ofshe proliferation more clearly. Accounting for choices of coalition partners is at the core of concern; "light guessing" simply provides a useful probabilistic framework for modeling the choice process. Sometimes the motivation is mixed, as seems to be the case in the Hannan and Freeman proliferation. Extending the ideas of population ecology into new areas seems to be at the core of their concern. However, there are specific issues in organizational theory they hope to be able to formulate more clearly with this approach. Specifically, using their "competition" models they hope to be able to account for some of the nonadaptive aspects of organizational growth.

Fertility is the most important criterion in the evaluation of proliferations. Does the proliferant theory generate new, researchable problems? Other criteria may, of course, be involved. However, their relevance is clearly subordinate; it is simply unnecessary to evaluate the rigor or simplicity of a theory if it does not provide any basis for further development.

Despite the prominence of a single criterion of evaluation in the assessment of proliferation, the assessment situation is not quite that simple. First, fertility is a notoriously difficult criterion of evaluation to explicate. Second, the evaluation is likely to be a long-term process; even if we know what fertility is, it is likely to require some time before the theory bears fruit. Thus, considerable development by other means (and evaluated by other criteria) is likely to be necessary before a clear evaluation of the success of a proliferation can be made. We cannot evaluate the success of any of the proliferations we have discussed without seeing where they take us. Elaborations and variations of those ideas (and evaluations of the success of those elaborations and variations) are necessary, therefore, before we can judge the fertility of a proliferation.

The choice situation presented by proliferation is dramatically different from that for any other type of relation. The explanatory domains of proliferant theories do not overlap. Hence, there is no comparative evaluation of the theories; neither is chosen because it is better than the other in some explanatory domain. Instead, the choice of $T(1)$ or $T(2)$ depends on what problem or phenomenon has been chosen for investigation. In no sense is Newcomb (1956) better than Heider (1944, 1946). Most important, the investigator cannot choose between them on the basis of relative empirical support. Instead, the choice must be based on the identification of an appropriate explanatory domain: cognitive organization or interpersonal attraction.

Branching best describes the growth process implied by proliferation. One theory draws on the resources of another theory to reach out to a new area. Proliferation is perhaps the most interesting kind of theory development. Certainly, it is one of the most creative and thought-provoking. It opens entirely new areas for a theorist to pursue; in effect, it provides a new path for the elaboration of theory. There has been very little discussion of proliferation in theory construction or the philosophy of science. This is unfortunate, since it is clearly a very important kind of growth. I will have much more to say about its importance in Chapter 5.

Integration

Integration presents a construction task very similar to elaboration. The task in this case is to unite two or more disparate formulations in a single theory while maintaining consistency with the original formulations. Again, as with elaboration, the objectives of integration are normally twofold: first, to reveal the interdependencies of T(1) and T(2) in T(3); second, to suggest some new ideas in T(3)—ones not already present in T(1) or T(2). Thus, Bacharach and Lawler (1981) reveal the interdependency of deterrence and conflict spiral theories by specifying the conditions of application for each.[23] The Bacharach and Lawler formulation also suggests new ideas (e.g., about concession behavior) not covered in either of the earlier theories.

The development of an integrating theory creates a distinct theoretical structure whose form depends on the nature of the relationship between the integrated theories. If T(1) and T(2) are variant theories, T(3) is likely to involve the *specification of conditions* for the application of each variant; T(1) is seen to apply under some circumstances, T(2) under others. This is what has occurred, for example, in Bacharach and Lawler's use of both conflict spiral and deterrence principles in their theory. The latter applies when stakes are low, the former when stakes are high. If T(1) and T(2) are proliferants, integration is more likely to entail the identification of properties that permit the *interrelation of disparate phenomena*. Such is the case (in at least a limited way) with the integration in Cook and Emerson (1978) of power and equity phenomena. Finally, if T(1) and T(2) are competitors, it is likely to require a new theoretical language (with new concepts) that enables the *selection and incorporation of principles* from each competitor in a coherent new formulation. Turner's (1975, 1982) theory of conflict represents an integration of the functionalist and Marxist approaches to conflict in just this way. Although his nine-step model captures some of the ideas in Coser's and Dahrendorf's theories, it does not directly correspond to the conceptual structures of either. Further, there are no direct parallels to his propositions about the interdependence of units in social systems or about the unequal distribution of scarce resources in either earlier theory.

In evaluating the success of any kind of integrating theory in revealing interdependencies, the theorist is concerned primarily with issues of comprehensiveness and compactness. Obviously, if too few of the problems covered by the earlier theories are included in the later theory, not much integration will take place. But more important, unless the later theory accounts for the problems with less theoretical apparatus than the earlier theories, the integration will be meaningless, for it is always possible to "integrate" two theories simply by conjoining them logically. Some sort of "condensation" must supplement the conjunction of two theories if integration is to represent any form of growth or development. Bacharach and Lawler use the *same* conceptual apparatus to conjoin deterrence and conflict spiral theory. As a result, their theory is more compact than the simple addition of one theory to another; hence, it is a valuable integration of the other two theories.

Evaluating the success of an integrating theory in generating new predictions may involve any of the criteria appropriate to elaboration. However, one criterion is particularly prominent. That criterion is "depth." Often the principles of an integrating theory are intended to be deeper, more basic, or more abstract than those of the theories being integrated. Deeper, more basic, more abstract principles should suggest deeper, more basic, more abstract predctions; if they do not, the integration is weakened.

Comprehensiveness, compactness, and depth are all reasonably complex criteria of evaluation. There are no automatic or simple procedures for evaluating theories on these criteria. Consequently, the assessment situation for integration is made more complicated simply on the basis of the kinds of criteria that are most prominent in evaluating the effort. The assessment situation becomes still more involved when we recall that integrations are likely to be only partial in most circumstances, as in the case of Cook and Emerson's (1978) integration of power/dependence and equity theory. Just how much comprehensiveness, compactness, or depth is needed to consider an integration successful is not likely to be easy to determine. For example, is the use of equity ideas in Cook and Emerson's work sufficiently central for that work to be considered a successful integration?

Further, to the extent that an integrating theory makes new predictions, those predictions must be evaluated empirically. Although this testing activity may be relatively straightforward, it is likely to take some time to complete. Generating and testing Bacharach and Lawler's bargaining theory has taken at least eight years and has involved at least eight separate studies. And, of course, much additional work can and should be done. Hence, judging the success of their integration has been a long-term process and is far from complete.

What is more, it is not at all clear how the theorist should proceed if the new predictions are not supported empirically. Should the integrating theory be scrapped, even though it successfully unites two other theories? Should the integrating theory be kept, even though it fails to go beyond the theories it unites? The choice is not a simple one, although it does seem likely to depend more frequently on the suggestiveness of the integrating theory than on the completeness of its coverage of T(1) and T(2).

The choice situation itself is, of course, much like the choice situation that arises in cases of elaboration. The difference here is that the integrating theory elaborates more than one theory. Which theory is chosen is likely to differ, depending on the relation between T(1) and T(2). If T(1) and T(2) are variants, then the integrating theory T(3) seems likely to be chosen almost universally (assuming the integration has been successful). The theories are so closely related that it is unlikely there is much information in the earlier theories that is not included in the later theory. This seems likely to be the ultimate outcome of the Bacharach and Lawler integration. Deterrence and conflict spiral are closely related variants, and the integrating theory encompasses most of the critical content of both theories.

If T(1) and T(2) are proliferants, theory choice seems likely to depend heavily on problem focus. A successful integrating theory will obviously be preferred in dealing with problems that are a part of the explanatory domain only because of the integration. However, one of the earlier theories may still be preferred in dealing with problems that were part of the domain *before* the integration occurred; the account provided by the earlier theory may be simpler, more direct, or more complete. This seems a more accurate description of the situation with regard to the Cook and Emerson integration. Power/dependence theory and equity theory are proliferants and the integration is minimal. Few interested in equity processes per se are likely to use the Cook and Emerson theory unless they are concerned specifically with the relationship between power and equity.

If T(1) and T(2) are competitors, theory choice may depend on the degree to which common grounds of evaluation can be identified. When such grounds can be identified, the choice situation is probably much like the situation when the earlier theories are proliferants; choice depends on problem focus. However, if there is very little agreement on grounds of evaluation, few are likely to prefer an integrating theory over the theories it integrates. The success and worth of the integration are likely to be subjects of considerable debate themselves. This is probably what dooms such integrative attempts as Denzin's (1969) "integration" of ideas from interactionism and ethnomethodology. The strategies simply do not share enough grounds of evaluation for attempts to integrate theories from the two different strategies to be successful. Obviously, the choice situation presented by integration can often be quite complex.

Integration is a *converging* type of growth. Previously unrelated ideas are shown to be closely related or similar in their implications by virtue of their integration in a single theory. Convergence is often seen as the ideal form of growth, paticularly by advocates of "the unity of science" and by advocates of a "general" theory of society. I suggest here, however, that convergence is simply one pattern of growth, not necessarily the ideal pattern.

To illustrate this difference, let us consider the Parsonian idea of convergence as it is developed in *The Structure of Social Action* (Parsons, 1937). First, for Parsons convergence was *inherent* in the work of Weber, Durkheim, Marshall, Pareto, and the other theorists he studied; that these theorists apparently were converging on the same general theory served as at least a partial validation of Parsons's work. Second, as a result, faithfulness to the work of these earlier theorists became an important criterion of evaluation in assessing the convergence Parsons proposed. Since most of these earlier theoretical works are best characterized as competitors, there has been much debate over the accuracy of Parsons's characterization (see, e.g., Cohen et al., 1975; Pope et al., 1975). Thus, evaluating the utility of the convergence Parsons attempted has become subordinate to evaluating the very fact of convergence. Further, the degree of ideological purity this appoach requires directly hinders any attempts to generate something theoretically "new," to *improve* our knowledge.

By contrast, the convergent pattern of growth I suggest here is in no sense presumed to be inherent in the theories that generate it. Further, such convergence is much more likely to involve variants or proliferants than competitors; the task of integration is simply much more manageable. Finally, convergence is not set up as the ideal for all theory growth. It is valuable and dramatic, but it is one pattern of many, each of which serves a different purpose.

Competition

Finally, we turn to competition, where the situation is the most complex of all. Basically, the task in competition is to capture another theory's explanatory domain. The objective is to replace the other theory by showing it to be a less satisfactory account of some problem or problems. This sort of goal is an imperialistic one; it involves the elimination of a competing conceptual framework (often one that has been generated from the perspective of a different orienting strategy). Neither Scheff nor Gove has been particularly interested in sharing the mental illness explanatory domain. Each theory assumes (and is intended to assume) that one kind of account of mental illness process is right and the other wrong.

There is very little agreement about what criteria are appropriate for the evaluation of competitors. Depending upon who is doing the evaluating, any or all criteria may be used. In fact, the only criterion about which there seems to be any agreement is relative empirical support, although even here questions of "what is empirical?" and "what is support?" are raised. This is certainly the case with respect to Gove's (1970) attack on and Scheff's (1974) defense of the labeling approach. Not only do they disagree about the *relevance* of much of the data, they also disagree about the *interpretation* of data they agree is relevant. The same results are interpreted as support by one and as nonsupport by the other.

Insofar as comparative empirical support for competitors can be evaluated, the assessment situation presented by competition is similar to the sort of assessment situation spelled out by Stinchcombe. However, in competition a great many other criteria of evaluation may be deemed relevant. Of course, proponents of each competitor are unlikely to agree about which criteria are relevant or about how to apply the criteria they agree are relevant. In short, the assessment situation for competitors is exceedingly complex. There is unlikely to be any settlement of the Scheff-Gove dispute in the foreseeable future.

Unsurprisingly, then, the choice situation that arises in competition is also hard to specify clearly. First, theory choice may depend largely on strategic assumptions; choices between competitors thus become much like choices between Kuhnian paradigms with all the complexities attendant thereto. Second, theory choice may also depend on the extent to which the explanatory domains of the theories overlap. If the overlap is only partial, the choice process is almost hopelessly snarled. Independent of "evidence," one may prefer Festinger's (1957) cognitive dissonance theory or Bem's (1964, 1967) self-perception theory, depending on whether one is cognitively or behaviorally oriented.

If the two theories differ in scope, precision, and the like,[24] how does one go about determining which theory is better? Even in the unlikely case that one theory is unambiguously better within the common domain, it is not possible to rule out the other theory as clearly a failure. For, as long as the overlap in domain is only partial, the "weaker" theory still explains *something* the other theory cannot. Only if the overlap in explanatory domains of the two theories is complete *and* the theorists can reach consensus on the criteria to be used in evaluating the theories comparatively *and* one theory is clearly better than the other by all these criteria is theory choice likely to be clear, unequivocal, and complete. These are, of course, almost impossible conditions to meet. Consequently, theory choice with competitors is normally a very long, very involved, very complex affair.

The process is made still more complex if a proliferant from an unrelated theory is involved as one of the competitors. Evaluation of the theory as a proliferant under these circumstances would appear to depend on the quality of its competitor (however that is determined), not just on its ability to generate interesting theoretical problems within the domain it explains. Evaluations of the theory as a competitor under these circumstances is likely to depend on the degree to which it is faithful to the theoretical structure from which it originated, not just on the explanatory advantages it may hold over its competitor.

Theory growth among competitors is generally a matter of *lateral accumulation* of findings. Each theory amasses a body of empirical support with very little building of one theory upon the other. This is only a very weak form of growth with little to recommend it. Further, there is a tendency for comparisons of competing theories to degenerate into metatheoretical disputes. Only if these disputes are resolved is there even a potential for the weak form of growth involved in lateral accumulation. Even under these conditions, growth depends on the completion of a long and difficult process of evaluation. Clearly, then, competition is not a very efficient form of theory growth.

GUIDING THEORY GROWTH

As I suggested at the beginning of this chapter, it is not possible to develop rules that will guarantee theoretical growth and development. It is possible, however, to identify and remove some of the obstacles to that development. In that spirit, I have a few suggestions for guiding theory development, based on the ideas I have presented thus far.

Distinguishing Theory from Metatheory

One of the most important obstacles to theory development is the failure adequately to distinguish different kinds of theoretical activity. As I demonstrated in Chapter 2, metatheoretical activity is quite different in character from theoretical activity; it therefore should be treated differently. There may, of course, be development in the structures of orienting strategies. However, the development is unlikely to be cumulative in any sense of the term, certainly not in the more limiting sense of linear progression.

In any case, the evaluation of strategies is based largely on nonscientific, directive criteria; strategy development is basically nonempirical. By contrast, theory development is presumed to involve empirical evaluation at some point. Thus, disputes that may arise in the attempt to develop theories are empirically resolvable, at least in principle. Such is not the case with disputes that arise in the attempt to develop strategies; most of these disagreements are unresolvable even in principle.

This suggests that we would be wise to spend much less time arguing over whether we ought to adopt a conflict or a consensus model of society, to assume a behavioral or cognitive view of interaction, or to pursue a Blumerian or Kuhnian style of symbolic interactionism. It further suggests that determining whether or not Parsons interpreted Weber or Durkheim correctly is largely wasted effort, at least with respect to the attempt to develop theoretical knowledge. Instead, we should spend a great deal more time actually developing the theories dictated by these metatheoretical positions.

To put it bluntly, it is time we stopped arguing over what sort of theory we ought to develop and got on with the task of actually developing that sort of theory!

Treating Theory Growth
as Multidimensional

Effectively pursuing the development of theory requires that we be aware of the details of the task we are about. First and foremost, this involves the realization that there are *multiple* paths to theory development. *There is no single method by which growth of theoretical knowledge can be assured.*

Almost as important is an understanding that each path of development entails a different theoretical task, assessed by different evaluative criteria. Ignoring these differences makes theory development much more difficult.

Consider proliferation, for example. Proliferant theories are not likely to be as precise, rigorous, or comprehensive as other theories, probably because the links between the original and the new explanatory domains are initially unclear. However, the success of a proliferant depends primarily on the fertility of its application to the new domain. Insistence that the proliferation be precise, rigorous, or comprehensive as well is likely to defeat the purpose of the proliferation—to reduce its fertility—and, hence, to constrain the *potential* for development along this path.

Consider also the example of variation. Variant theories are likely to be quite limited and technical in their focus, since they are designed to focus on a single issue (or a very small number of issues) distinguishing them. Criticizing either theory because of its narrowness of application is inappropriate, since it is exactly that narrowness that is needed to enable resolution of the issue or issues. The theorist is often attempting to determine exactly how the larger theory is to be articulated. The basic structure of that larger theory is not at issue; the mode of articulation is. Again, misapplying criteria of evaluation hinders the potential for development along this path.

An awareness that some patterns do not really promote development is also important. In particular, competition is by far the most difficult sort of growth to evaluate. In fact, if the competing theories are based on different orienting strategies, some of the conflicts between the theories may be unresolvable. Growth may not occur at all, and if it does, it is likely to proceed very slowly. By contrast, although elaboration, variation, proliferation, and integration are sometimes quite complex tasks, they are seldom as fraught with difficulty as is competition. Certainly, since each of these four tasks is attempted within a shared theoretical structure, it is unlikely that theoretical problems will be unresolvable in principle. In any case, elaboration, variation, proliferation, and integration ought to be considered much more fruitful avenues of theoretical development than is competition; therefore, they ought to be pursued with considerably more fervor than competition.

Systematically Pursuing Growth

It is possible to pursue a coordinated program of development, involving all four of the more fruitful types of development. Such programs may be called *theoretical research programs.* I believe that theoretical research programs provide considerably more opportunity for theory growth and development than do any of the specific types of development individually.

Further, the interaction among the types of development within a program is likely to generate still more development. I therefore argue that the program constitutes the most appropriate context within which to evaluate and encourage theory growth and development.

The purpose of Chapter 5, then, is to explicate the program notion. What are its elements? How do these elements relate to the types of development I have already identified? How does one go about evaluating a program? Most important, how does the pursuit of a theoretical research program contribute to the development of sociological knowledge?

Chapter 5

Theoretical Research Programs

THE BASIC CLAIM

Elaboration, variation, proliferation, and integration all contribute individually to the growth and development of theoretical knowledge. In addition, some of these relations often interact with others in making a contribution. Consider, for example, integration. The theories that become integrated are variants or proliferants (or conceivably even competitors) with respect to each other. Further, the act of integration is an elaboration of both of the earlier theories. Consider also variation. If we assume that the conflict between the variants is not immediately resolved, then both variants are likely to be elaborated in an effort to spell out more clearly the nature of the differences between them. Consider proliferation. Laying claim to an explanatory domain is only the first step in developing the account of that domain. Determining the ultimate value of any proliferant, therefore, depends heavily on articulating its explanatory accounts through elaboration, variation, and so on.

Thus, it would seem reasonable to consider the *collective* contribution of these relations to theory growth and development, particularly when they are pursued systematically. This sort of systematic effort to develop theoretical knowledge creates a *theoretical research program* (TRP). Let us initially define a theoretical research program as a set of related theories together with relevent research. With this basic conception in mind, we can turn to more specific questions about the nature and consequences of such programs. What does a TRP look like? How do the various types of relations fit into the TRP concept? How do we evaluate the development of TRPs?

AN EXAMPLE

There are many theoretical research programs in sociology. For example, most of the illustrations in Chapter 3 are drawn from TRPs. The functional theory of stratification, mobility models, balance theory, transitivity theory, ecological models of organization, power/dependence theory, strain theories of deviance, equity theory, the labeling theory of mental illness, coalition formation theory, and bargaining theory all have been pursued programmatically.

However, in this chapter I will focus on a program not included in that list: expectation states theory. The reasons for the choice are several. First, more than many other programs, expectation state theory illustrates *all* the types of relations. Second, it is a program with which I have been personally involved. Therefore, I am considerably more familiar with its course of development than with that of any other program. Finally, my knowledge of the expectation states program has been helpful in explicating the ideas I have been presenting in this monograph. Consequently, in many ways expectation states theory is best suited for demonstrating the points I wish to make.[25]

The Expectation States Program

THE INITIAL IDEA

The expectation states theoretical research program originated in the doctoral dissertation of Joseph Berger, completed in 1957. Berger was primarily interested in providing a theoretical explanation for some of the empirical regularities observed by Bales in small, informal, problem-solving groups whose members were initially equally in status. Specifically, Berger was interested in accounting for three of Bales's basic results:

(1) Inequalities in amount of interaction initiated, in amount of interaction received, in evaluations of individual performances, and in influence over the group's decisions all emerge very rapidly in such groups.

(2) All of these inequalities are highly correlated with each other.

(3) Once the inequalities emerge in the group, they tend to be maintained throughout the course of the group's interaction; a group's hierarchy tends to become stable.

In his explanation for these regularities Berger began with an idealized description of the interaction process in Bales's groups. Basically, an actor is granted an *action opportunity* (a chance to initiate interaction); given an action opportunity, the actor may then make a *performance output* (initiate interaction); once an actor has performed, others in the group communicate *unit evaluations* of that performance (positive or negative judgments of the quality of the actor's contribution); finally, given these evaluations, the actors exert more or less *influence* over each other with respect to the group's decisions.

Together, these four behaviors constitute what Berger referred to as the *observable power and prestige order* of the group. It is the emergence, consistency, and stability of this ordering that Berger sought to explain.

The argument Berger developed is based on an *evaluation/expectation* process. Specifically, actors make unit evaluations of their own and each others' past performances. Over time, these evaluations may often come to be rather consistent. The more consistent the evaluations of the performances of a particular actor are, the more likely it is that the members of the group will develop *expectation states* (anticipations for future performance) for that actor. Once these expectations emerge, all later unit evaluations (as well as the other observable power and prestige behaviors) are based on the expectations, rather than on actual performance, for that actor.

Thus are the Bales results explained. First, the inequalities emerge as a result of the differential evaluations of past performances for the various members of the group. Second, the inequalities are highly correlated as a result of the determination of the observable power and prestige behaviors by expectations. Finally, the inequalities are maintained because the evaluations and the expectations (once they emerge) are mutually reinforcing. Expectations determine unit evaluations; unit evaluations in turn confirm expectations.

THE POWER AND PRESTIGE BRANCH

The basic principles of the evaluation/expectation process have been explored in more detail in a branch of the expectation states program known as "power and prestige theory."

First, Berger and Conner (1969) developed a more detailed description of the interaction process in terms of cycles of power and prestige behaviors. Their theory identified parameters specifying the likelihood that a particular kind of behavior (e.g., performance output or negative unit evaluation) would occur in a particular interaction cycle. In addition, using this theory, it became possible to derive probabilities for the occurrence of each power and prestige behavior in a particular actor's interaction, given the establishment of expectations for that actor.

These ideas were expanded in Berger and Conner (1974). This formulation developed a more comprehensive description of the interaction process, including the emergence of expectations as an element in that process. As a consequence of this characterization, the revised formulation allowed for the possibility of differences in behavioral dispositions for each actor in the absence of established expectations.

The ideas in these theories have been generally well-supported by research. (See, especially, the research results reported in Berger et al., 1974: Part 1.) Most of the studies have been laboratory experiments in which actors are asked to make unit evaluations of their own and others' contributions to an ambiguous decision-making task. Differences in influence behavior are then predicted on the basis of differences in the unit evaluations made.[26]

THE STATUS CHARACTERISTICS BRANCH

Ideas in this branch of the program are concerned in large part with some results emerging from the extensive small groups literature of the 1950s (e.g., Torrance, 1954; Caudill, 1958; Strodtbeck et al., 1958). Specifically, that literature showed that external status differences determine the distribution of power and prestige behaviors in task groups, even when the status involved is unrelated to the task. Explanation of this generalization became the goal of a branch of the program known as status characteristics theory.

Status characteristics theory posits a *status/expectation* process, parallel to the evaluation/expectation process. In the latter, expectations emerge from the unit evaluations of actors who are initially equal in status. In the former, expectations emerge from the status information that differentiates actors initially. In both, expectations then determine the distribution of power and prestige behaviors in the group.

The first formulation in this branch of the program (Berger et al., 1966) covered situations in which information from only one status characteristic is available to the actors. That characteristic was assumed to be diffuse in its implications (i.e., applicable across a broad range of situations, as is often the case with characteristics like sex or race). Under such circumstances, the theory argued, the burden of proof is on demonstrating that the status information is irrelevant to the group's interaction. That is, the status information will be used to generate expectations for performance of the group's task, unless the actors have a specific reason for believing the information is irrelevant. Thus, in accord with the generalization, external (i.e., diffuse) status information determines power and prestige in the group, even when the status information is irrelevant to the task. The only circumstance in which it does not do so is when the actors explicitly believe it to be irrelevant.

This version of status characteristics theory has been strongly supported by data. Again, most of the studies have been experimental. Initial status differences are manipulated and differences in influence behavior—i.e., in levels of P(S)—are predicted.

Berger and Fisek (1974) extended the original status characteristics theory considerably. Most important, they expanded coverage of the theory to multicharacteristic situations involving any number of characteristics of a variety of types. These types included the diffuse characteristics already mentioned, specific characterisitics (i.e., characteristics that have implications only with respect to a particular task), and goal objects (i.e., elements in the situation with reward significance).

The most important issue that arises in multicharacteristic situations concerns status inconsistency. How is inconsistent status information organized into expectations? At least two general kinds of answers are possible. First, actors may "eliminate" some of the information, basing their expectations only on a consistent subset of the available information. Second, actors may "combine" all of the information, using both consistent and inconsistent information in developing expectations.

Berger and Fisek suggested combining. Research on the issue has been extensive (see, e.g., Kervin, 1974; Freese and Cohen, 1973; Zelditch et al., 1975; Webster and Driskell, 1978). The results of this research generally support combining; however, a number of plausible circumstances under which eliminating may occur have not yet been explored.

The first two status characteristics theory formulations deal with situations involving only two actors. Using ideas from Berger and Fisek (1974) and from Kervin (1974), Berger, Fisek, and Norman (1977) expanded consideration to situations involving more than two actors. In addition, they formalized the argument using graph theory. One of the most important consequences of this formalization is that it becomes possible to derive interval ordering predictions for P(S) (i.e., influence) behavior, not just the basic ordering predictions previously derivable.

Some recent studies support this latest theory (see, e.g., Riznek, 1977; Knottnerus and Greenstein, 1981; Wagner and Ford, 1983). However, a great deal of testing remains to be done.

THE DISTRIBUTIVE JUSTICE BRANCH

The ideas in the distributive justice branch of expectation states theory are rooted in a challenge to equity theory (see the discussion of Homans

[1974] and Adams [1965] in Chapter 3). Basically, equity theory argues that justice evaluations are based on comparisons of one actor's actual reward situation with that of another. By contrast, the "status value theory" developed in this branch (Berger, Zelditch, Anderson, and Cohen, 1972) argues that justice evaluations are based on comparisons of an actor's actual reward situation with the reward situation he or she expects. In turn, these reward expectations are based on referential norms and standards for reward distribution (called referential structures).

If the reward allocation an actor actually receives matches expectations, the situation is seen as just; otherwise, it is assessed as unjust. With this characterization it becomes possible to identify a variety of justice assessments, including many that cannot be represented in equity theory. For example, overreward can be clearly distinguished from underreward; self-injustice can be distinguished from other-injustice and, perhaps most important, individual injustice can be distinguished from collective injustice.

Status value theory generates a *referential structure/reward expectation* process. Again, the process is parallel to the evaluation/expectation and status/expectation processes, except that here the expectations involved concern rewards rather than task performance capabilities. Thus, information from referential structures determines reward expectations; these expectations then determine reward allocation (or reallocation) behavior.

Partial support for the status value theory has been generated (see, e.g., Cook, 1975; Webster and Smith, 1978). However, efforts to test the theory have been limited by a methodological problem involving demand characteristics. Basically, two alternative interpretations of reward behavior in these situations are available.

(1)   Actors base their expectations on the referential structure(s) activated in the situation.

(2)   Actors base their expectations on what the experimenter has told them to expect (when he or she attempts to introduce referential structure information into the situation).

Berger et al. (1983) have developed a formulation that may solve this problem. This theory extends the ideas in the latest status characteristics theory (Berger, Fisek, and Norman, 1977) to include both performance expectations and reward expectations. The two are seen as interdependent; therefore, the behaviors based on these expectations are also seen as interdependent. As a consequence, the theory permits predictions of the effect of reward expectations on task behavior (and also of the effect of task expectations on reward behavior). Thus, it is possible to test the effects of referential structures on task behavior, rather than on reward behavior; since the experimenter says nothing about task behavior in introducing the referential structure, the alternative explanation can be ruled out. Tests of these ideas are currently under way.

In other recent work Jasso (1978) has developed a new approach to justice issues that incorporates elements of both status value theory and equity theory. Jasso points out many of the weaknesses of both earlier theories. For example, she criticizes the equity approach for its inability to distinguish overreward from underreward consistently and to handle collective injustice (whether involving overreward or underreward) at all. She also suggests a major weakness in status value theory. Specifically, she points out that the equation used there results in justice evaluations that are stated in terms of units of the particular reward commodity, rather than in units of "justice." The latter is necessary, she argues, if a comprehensive theory of distributive justice is to be developed.

Jasso then rearranges the equity and status value equations as a step in her development of a *justice evaluation function* that can be applied to any socially distributed good. In equity theory, for example,

$$\text{justice evaluation} = \text{A's reward/A's investment} - \text{B's reward/B's investment} \qquad [1]$$

whereas, for status value theory,

$$\text{justice evaluation} = \text{actual reward} - \text{just reward} \qquad [2]$$

Jasso's generalized justice evaluation function is then specified as

$$\text{justice evaluation} = \ln(\text{actual amount of good/just amount of good}) \qquad [3]$$

That is, an evaluation of the justice of a reward distrubution is a function of the natural logarithm of the ratio of an actor's actual rewards to the rewards he or she assesses as just. Alternatively, the evaluation may be seen as the difference between the logarithms of the actual and just amount, which is mathematically equivalent. Jasso supposes that equity theorists would be more likely to prefer the logarithm of the ratio, while status value theorists would prefer the difference between two logarithms. However, since the forms are mathematically equivalent, the justice evaluation function has adequately captured critical features of both theories.

Jasso makes no attempt in her theory to cover all the explanatory domain of the two earlier theories. For example, equity theorists are frequently concerned with predicting specific means of redressing an injustice. Jasso makes no predictions in this respect. Similarly, status value theory makes predictions regarding the assessment of situations where the injustice involves only others. Jasso specifically excludes this issue from her conceptualization.

Jasso's theory does make some predictions not made by either the equity or status value theories. For example, the use of a logarithm results in a weighting that makes underreward more keenly felt than overreward, a phenomenon all justice theorists have assumed occurred, but which has not previously been incorporated in their theories.

Jasso elaborates her argument considerably in Jasso (1980). Among other things, she separates evaluations involving "quality goods" (e.g., beauty) from those involving "quantity goods" (e.g., salary) and considers the application of the justice evaluation function to more than one good at a time. She also develops a *justice evaluation distribution* within a social or conceptual aggregate by assuming consensus about the goods valued within the aggregate. A variety of empirically testable hypotheses are then suggested relating properties of the distribution to particular social conditions (e.g., to rates of crime and mental illness).

THE SOURCES OF EVALUATION BRANCH

Theoretical work in this branch of the program is intended to capture ideas about the effects of significant others on an actor's self-evaluations. This work, called source theory, treats significant others as "sources" (individuals viewed as more capable than one's self in evaluating performances). The likelihood that a particular evaluator will become a source for an actor is based on that actor's expectations for the evaluator; the higher the expectations, the more likely the evaluator is to become a source. Once a source has emerged, his or her evaluations determine the actor's self-evaluations (which, in turn, determine expectations and behavior).

The *source/expectation* process specified in source theory is, of course, parallel to the processes specified in the theories in the other branches of the program. Here source evaluations determine unit evaluations of self, which determine expectations, which determine behavior.

Webster (1969) provided the first account of this process, focusing only on cases in which one source evaluator is present. His experiment strongly supported that account.

Sobieszek (1972) extended the argument to multiple source situations. As in the status characteristics branch, the inconsistency issue becomes salient in multiple source situations. How do actors deal with inconsistent evaluations from two or more sources? Again, both "eliminating" (e.g., ignore one source) and "combining" (e.g., distribute self-evaluations among conflicting sources) alternatives are possible.

Sobieszek assumed that actors would ignore evaluations from *all* conflicting sources. Her data supported this assumption. However, later research by Webster, Roberts, and Sobieszek (1972) showed that actors actually distribute evaluations among conflicting sources. Again, combining seems to be the more common method for handling inconsistent information.

Webster and Sobieszek (1974) incorporated this result (and a few others) in a restatement of the theory. This formulation involved no major revisions; rather it refined and coordinated the previous results. Although no new formulation of source theory has been developed since 1974, research continues in this branch (see, e.g., Crundall and Foddy, 1981).

PATTERNS OF GROWTH IN THE EXPECTATION STATES PROGRAM

Each of the types of relations I have discussed is evident in the development of the expectation states theoretical research program. Elaboration, for example, is evident in the relations among the three versions of status characteristics theory. Specifically, Berger and Fisek (1974) is an elaboration of Berger et. al. (1966); and Berger, Fisek, and Norman (1977) is an elaboration of Berger and Fisek (1974). In each case the elaborant provides accounts of more complex situations than the earlier theory. Berger and Fisek consider situations involving any number and kind of status characteristics, while the original theory considers only single characteristic situations; Berger, Fisek, and Norman account for the behavior of any number of actors, while the earlier theory accounts for the behavior of only two. Furthermore, each elaborant makes more precise predictions (and hence allows a more precise fit to the data) than the earlier theory, moving progressively from the basic ordering predictions of the original theory to the interval ordering predictions of Berger, Fisek, and Norman. Finally, the elaborants are more rigorously formulated; in particular, Berger, Fisek, and Norman is much more formalized than is Berger and Fisek.

Elaboration is also evident in the relation between Webster (1969) and Sobieszek (1972) in source theory. Here, of course, the elaboration is much less extensive than in status characteristics theory; the major change introduced by Sobieszek is a consideration of multiple sources, not just the single source Webster considered.

Perhaps the best example of variation in the expectation states program is in the relation between Berger and Fisek (1974) and Kervin (1974) in status characteristics theory. The problem foci are identical. The theoretical structures are very similar. However, Berger and Fisek assume that ''equating'' information (information that actors have the same status) is generally ignored; Kervin assumes it is taken into account in forming expectations. In most situations the predictions of the two theories are identical; only when equating information is involved do the predictions conflict.

A less complete example of variation is the relation between Berger and Fisek (1974) and Freese and Cohen (1973).[27] Implicitly, the two theories share many assumptions (e.g., about how status information comes into play); however, they differ explicitly in their accounts of how status information gets organized into expectations. Specifically, Berger and Fisek assume that all status information is combined into an ''averaged'' expectation state, while Freese and Cohen assume that, under some conditions, some status information is eliminated, yielding a ''balanced'' high or low expectation state. As a consequence, when inconsistent status information is present, the former predicts intermediate P(S) values (i.e., levels of influence), while the latter predicts more extreme values. When only consistent information is involved, the predictions of the two theories are identical.

Each branch of the program represents proliferation. Theories in all the branches share much of their theoretical structure—the notion of an expectation state and the assumption that expectations determine power and prestige behaviors, to name but two. However, the theories in each branch are directed to the solution of very different problems. Power and prestige theories deal with interaction in initially status-equal groups. Status characteristics theories deal with the effects of status differentiation (and status inconsistency) on task behavior. Status value theories deal with issues of justice and injustice. Source theories deal with the effects of significant others on one's self-evaluations. Hence, there is little overlap in predictions between theories in different branches of the program; they are simply concerned with different phenomena.

Although pure cases of integration are probably quite rare, three partial examples can be identified in the expectation states program. First, Berger, Fisek, and Norman (1977) represents an integration of two variant theories—Berger and Fisek (1974) and Kervin (1974). While the integrating theory incorporates much more of the language of Berger and Fisek than it does of Kervin, it does introduce concern for issues that originally were considered only in the Kervin theory. For example, Kervin was much more concerned with differences in the strength of expectations in different situations than were Berger and Fisek. Kervin also considered the effects of equating information that Berger and Fisek had assumed would be ignored. The integrating theory dealt with these differences in two different ways. First, differences in strength of expectations were incorporated directly in the structure of the theory. Second, conditions were specified for when equating status information would be used and when it would not (thus stating the conditions under which the arguments of each of the two earlier theories should apply).

Another example of partial integration appears in Berger et al. (1983), which considers issues that were first raised separately in status characteristics theory (Berger, Zelditch, Anderson, and Cohen, 1972). Since it unites theoretical arguments originally directed to different sociological problems (i.e., status organization and distributive justice), the new theory represents an integration of proliferants. The integration is only partial, however, because some of the predictions in the status value theory (particularly about how referential structures emerge) are not covered in the new formulation. In addition, new predictions are made about the interdependence of task and reward expectations.

Integration of competitors is represented by Jasso (1978, 1980). Her integration involves recasting both arguments in terms of justice evaluation functions and showing how forms of both can be incorporated in a more sophisticated log function. As a consequence, the predictions she makes encompass many—but far from all—the issues in the explanatory domains of the earlier theories. (For instance, she has nothing to say about injustices involving others.) Further, she makes some predictions not made in either equity or status value theory. (For instance, she predicts differential effects of over and underreward.)

Clearly, given the example just cited, one instance of competition in the expectation states program is the relation between status value theory (Berger, Zelditch, Anderson, and Cohen, 1972) and equity theory (e.g., Adams, 1965). Their problem foci are similar and their structures dissimilar. Although there are many differences in predictions, there are some areas of agreement. Thus, this instance of competition represents a relatively moderate example of the relation (which may help to account for Jasso's success in developing a useful integration of the two).

Clearly, as the expectation states example shows, theory development can be pursed programmatically, using each of the types of relations I have identified. But can we say anything more specific about the character of theoretical research programs? What effects, for example, does each of the types of relations have on the character and growth of the program? Before we attempt to answer these questions, we need to define the properties of a TRP a little more clearly.

THE DEFINING CHARACTERISTICS OF A
THEORETICAL RESEARCH PROGRAM

The properties of a TRP are defined in terms of a series of *anatomical sets*. These sets represent parameters within which theory growth may occur in a TRP; program growth may be described, therefore, as a change in the value of one or more of those parameters.

The Formal Sets

TRPs are sets of related theories. The most important basis of the relations among those theories is structural; all or almost all the theories in a program share conceptual and propositional elements. The *core* set of a TRP is composed of just these elements. In contrast, there are other structural features that are not shared by all the theories in the program. These elements comprise the *auxiliary* set of a TRP. Together, these sets may be described as the *formal* sets of a TRP.

The formal sets may be differentiated by more than their frequency of appearance. First, the core set is more central to the program than is the auxiliary set. The elements of the core set are those concepts and assertions deemed essential for the construction of an adequate explanation of a particular social process. Elements may be included in the core set for a variety of reasons (e.g., because metatheoretical directives of an orienting strategy dictate their inclusion or because past attempts to explain the process without using those elements have all failed). The reasons behind inclusion are not particularly important, since the consequences are always the same: Some set of concepts and assertions comes to be seen as critical, essential, basic to the conceptualization and explanation of a given social process. This is the core set of a program. Auxiliary set elements, then, are concepts and assertions deemed less critical or basic. They support or elaborate the basic theoretical argument but could be replaced without altering the basic structure of explanation or rendering it generally inadequate.

Core and auxiliary elements can also be differentiated in terms of the consequences of their exposure to empirical evaluation. In general, auxiliary set elements are more likely to be rejected as a result of empirical evaluations than are core set elements. That is, since some concepts and assertions are less important to the statement of a theory than are others, it is reasonable to suggest that some of these concepts and assertions (auxiliary set elements) may be doubted before others (core set elements).

Of course, if alteration or replacement of auxiliary set elements fails to yield support, at some point the theorist will have to reevaluate the core concepts and assertions and perhaps give up the theory. Thus, the core set of a TRP is not immune from falsification, but merely resistant to it.[28]

The most basic defining characteristic of a theoretical research program is the presence of a core set; it is the most important way in which theories in a program are related.

Program growth may occur through either of two basic types of changes in the formal sets of a program: (1) in the composition of the sets or (2) in the organization, clarity, or refinement of elements already in the set. Compositional changes usually involve the addition of elements to the set; in the core set this generally means the addition of an element previously in the auxiliary set as it becomes more important to the formulation of theories in the program; however, compositional changes in the auxiliary set are more likely to involve the addition of elements not previously used in any theory in the program. In the former case the addition frequently indicates a generalization of the basic argument to include more aspects of the social process being explained (i.e., an increase in scope). In the latter case the addition generally represents an extension of the basic argument to deal with a different social process (i.e., an increase in range).

By contrast, changes in organization, clarity, or refinement of elements of either of the formal sets may involve, for example, the removal of logical inconsistencies, definition of primitive terms, formalization of the theoretical argument, or the elaboration or ''stretching'' of the meaning of a concept. No new elements are introduced. Instead, the ''character'' of elements that are already members of the set is altered; properties of elements are added, deleted, changed, expanded, or refined.

The Formal Sets of the Expectation States Program

One basic concept and two kinds of assertions compose the core set of expectation states theory. The concept is, of course, the notion of an expectation state. This concept is particularly important as a link between the two kinds of core assertions in the program.

The first of those assertions—an "emergence of expectations" assertion—specifies the process (or processes) by which a particular kind or source of cognitive information in a given situation becomes organized into a stable structure of expectations for actors in that situation. Thus, for example, in the power and prestige branch, the assertion specifies an evaluation/expectation process; in the status characteristics branch a status/expectations process is specified; and so on.

The second core assertion serves to relate established expectations to behavior—an "effects of expectation states" assertion. In most branches of the program this assertion deals with the effects of expectations on one or more of the power and prestige behaviors: action opportunities, performance outputs, communicated unit evaluations, and influence. However, in the distributive justice branch the assertion is concerned primarily with the effects of expectations on reward behavior, not one of the power and prestige behaviors.

As the program has developed, the changes in the core set have been extensive. First, the properties of the expectation states concept have become more clearly and precisely identified. Further, the concept has been elaborated and "stretched" to deal with more theoretical issues. Thus, for example, early in the program, as its basic ideas were being worked out, expectation states were understood simply as actors' beliefs about their own and others' performance capabilities. Later, as the power and prestige branch developed, theories came to include also a more specific sense of expectations as actors' anticipations for future performance. Then, as the status characteristics branch expanded, the concept became still further stretched, incorporating expectations aggregated from the status information available to the actors.

Different kinds of expectations have also been identified. For example, work in three of the branches has been concerned with expectations for task performance. With the development of the distributive justice branch of the program, the expectation states concept has been further expanded to include the actor's expectations for reward allocation as well.

Stretching of the "emergence" assertion has occurred in conjunction with the development of each branch of the program. Each new branch has incorporated a different kind or source of cognitive information available to the actor to be organized into expectations. Thus, expectations have been progressively seen to emerge from (1) unit evaluations, (2) status differences, (3) referential structures, and (4) sources of evaluation, as described in each branch of the program.

Modifications in the "effects" assertion have been equally extensive. For example, Berger and Fisek (1974) indicated that power and prestige behaviors are a function of an actor's expectation *advantage* over the other. This refinement permits accommodation of a variety of interval differences in expectations bearing on the same ordinal relationship. Thus, the status characteristics theories could now consider not only whose expectations are higher, but how much higher they are, in determining the power and prestige order of the group.

Overall, then, the elements of the core set of expectation states theory have become much more general in application; they have also become clearer and more precise (at least as they are used in some branches of the program).

A very large number of concepts and assertions have become elements of the auxiliary set of the expectation states program. In general, these elements have been introduced and used widely in one branch of the program. Sometimes these elements have then become incorporated in other branches.

Thus, for example, the notions of diffuse and specific status characteristics and of goal objects were introduced in status characteristics theory by Berger and Fisek (1974). That same theory also introduced a "combining" mechanism for dealing with inconsistent status information. The combining mechanism was later added to source theory by Webster, Roberts, and Sobieszek (1972). The referential structures idea was introduced in status value theory by Berger, Zelditch, Anderson, and Cohen (1972). The source idea was introduced in source theory by Webster (1969).

Most of these elements are relatively important in the formulation of theories within a particular branch of the program. In a sense, they constitute the core sets of the branches in which they are used. There are, however, a great many other auxiliary set elements whose role is almost entirely to help fill out the arguments made in each theory. These elements are auxiliary even within the branches in which they are used.

Overall, a large number of concepts and assertions has been added to the auxiliary set of the expectation states program as each new branch has emerged. In addition, many of the concepts and assertions have been revised or replaced to permit a more general (and sometimes more precise) account of the processes they describe in later formulations in the appropriate branches.

The Heuristic Set

In general, auxiliary set elements in a program are not introduced randomly; they are not arbitrarily chosen. Instead, auxiliary set elements are introduced to accomplish one of two purposes; they are used (1) to enable the application of the theory to some problem, phenomenon, or explanatory domain it previously did not cover or (2) to permit the generation of a more comprehensive account of a problem, phenomenon, or explanatory domain already covered by the theory on a less complex level. A third parameter of theory growth can therefore be identified. The theories in a program are directed to the formulation of particular theoretical problems they propose to solve. In other words, theories serve a heuristic purpose; they are tools for the explanation of some range of phenomenal situations. The *heuristic* set of a program can therefore be characterized as the set of substantive problems formulated using the formal sets of a theoretical research program.

Inclusion in the heuristic set requires only that the problem be formulated in the program, not necessarily that it be already solved. What is critical for growth is that theories may potentially solve a theoretical problem; it is not required that they actually have solved them.

The heuristic set of a TRP is concerned with issues of the scope and range of theories in the program. The scope of application of a theory is determined by the comprehensiveness of its account of a particular social process or phenomenon. Thus, changes in scope in the heuristic set may sometimes coincide with compositional changes in the core set. However, few changes in scope are as radical as would be required to alter the composition of the core set. Most of the time, scope changes are likely to involve such alterations as an increase in the number of social units for whose behavior the theory seeks to account.

The range of a TRP is determined by the breadth or quantity of different processes or phenomena for which the formal sets of the program enable the theorist to formulate explanations. Changes in the range in the heuristic set are quite frequently associated with changes in the composition of the auxiliary set. As new problems are introduced in the heuristic set of the program, new concepts and assertions are introduced in the auxiliary set to permit an extension of the basic theoretical argument to formulate an account of the new problem.

In any case, identification of the heuristic set of a program permits the evaluation of possible changes from $T(1)$ to $T(2)$ in the range of phenomena accounted for or in the comprehensiveness of a particular account. One can first determine if the range or scope has changed, and, if it has changed, in what ways it has changed.

The Heuristic Set of the
Expectation States Program

The range of problems formulated in the expectations states program is essentially equivalent to the set of issues considered across the various branches of the program. Thus, the range of problems includes the emergence and maintenance of power and prestige orders in small groups, the effect of status information on social interaction, the effect of referential reward information on assessments of justice, and the effect of the evaluations of significant others on one's self-evaluation. These problems were formulated in expectation states terms approximately in the order listed.

Clearly, the range of problems in the heuristic set has grown significantly. The initial element of the heuristic set was the problem of the emergence and maintenance of power and prestige orders. Three new problems have since been added to the set.

The scope of the explanations of each of these problems is, of course, specific to each branch. In the status characteristics branch, for example, scope has expanded from consideration of situations involving two actors differentiated with respect to one diffuse status characteristic, through situations involving any number and kind of characteristics, to situations involving any number of actors and characteristics. In the sources of evaluation branch, scope increases have primarily involved consideration of multiple sources, not just one. In the power and prestige branch, scope changes have involved the inclusion of more steps in the interaction process (e.g., the emergence, not just the effects, of expectations).

Certainly, the increase in the scope of formulations in the status characteristics branch has been much greater than in any other branch of the program.

The Observational Set

Theories propose solutions to the problems they formulate. The ways in which these solutions are evaluated are quite important. First, it is obviously important that a theory be capable of evaluation; it is further important that there be some means of comparing evaluations of different theories in a program if growth is to occur. To the extent that observational techniques and standards are held in common throughout the program, it is more readily possible to evaluate whether conflicting results can be attributed to observational problems or must be attributed to some other cause. For if a theory is tested in different empirical situations with similar observational techniques, it is more difficult to argue that those techniques were not a problem in a successful test, but that the same techniques were a problem in an unsuccessful test. Further, the character of the data base of relevant observations is also quite important. Obviously, the degree of support provided by that base is important, but other issues may also arise. Have the findings been, or are they capable of, replication? Are empirical findings surprising or novel in quality? Have there been challenges to the relevance of some portion of the data base or the nature of the inferences made from the data base? How well have these challenges been handled?

Certainly each of these issues is important in understanding growth. They suggest another parameter that identifies important characteristics of growth in a TRP—the *observational* set, which includes the following:

(1)   the observational techniques, procedures, inference rules, and standards used in evaluating theories in the program;

(2)   the data base of relevant observations; and

(3)   evaluations of the data base and its relevance to the theories in the program.

The elements of the observational set permit analysis of three basic empirical issues that affect growth of theories in a program. The first of these issues is the coherence of the data base (i.e., the degree to which observational techniques, procedures, and the like, permit systematic evaluation of the empirical support of theories). The second is the consistency of the data base (i.e., the degree to which empirical evaluations in fact support the predictions of theories). The third is the relevance of the data base (i.e., the degree to which empirical evaluations constitute legitimate evidence for or against theories).

Traditionally, discussion of the empirical utility of theories has focused almost exclusively on the second of these issues, the consistency of the data base. The more highly confirmed the theory, the more useful it is usually assumed to be. While confirmation status is obviously a critical issue, it is no more and no less important than the coherence and relevance of those confirming instances. In fact, a determination of the consistency of a data base with a theory (i.e., of the confirmation status of the theory) *depends* on a determination of the coherence and relevance of the data base.

Clearly, the more systematically one is able to evaluate consistency, the more reliable that evaluation will be. Further, as coherence increases, the more immediately and precisely the theorist can identify what theoretical changes would be required to resolve any inconsistency with the data base.

Vague or unsystematic observational techniques, rules, and standards permit inconsistencies to be interpreted in a multitude of different ways. Increased coherence of the evaluation of the data base rules out many of those interpretations.

Specification of the relevance of the data base to a theory determines the validity of any evaluations of consistency made. It makes no difference how consistently the data *seem* to support the theory if the data are not even relevant to the theory. Consistency becomes important only to the extent that the evaluations can be assumed to be valid, relevant comparisons of theory and data. For example, studies relating race and intelligence usually assume that IQ tests provide a valid and reliable measure of intelligence. If, as is frequently argued, IQ tests are an invalid measure of intelligence, it makes no difference what correlation is found between race and IQ; the results will be uninformative about the relationship between race and intelligence.

Changes in the composition or character of elements of the observational set may, of course, affect any or all of these issues. In fact, as the discussion above suggests, changes in the observational techniques (which affect coherence) or the addition of challenges to the value of those techniques (which affect relevance) almost always alter the confirmation status of the data base (which affects consistency). Although changes in the character of elements in the observational set are not, in general, tied to any one kind of change in the heuristic or formal sets, data-base changes may lead to, result from, or even prevent changes in at least one of those sets. For example, a challenge to the relevance of some portion of the data base may call into question the adequacy of the account of a particular process, which may, in turn, prevent any increases in the scope of that account until relevant data can be obtained.

In addition, a more explicit or formal statement of the core elements of a program may permit a more coherent and systematic evaluation of the data base. For example, as a theoretical concept becomes more precisely defined, it usually becomes possible to determine more adequately whether or not a particular concrete event represents an instance of that abstract concept.

The Observational Set of the Expectation States Program

Although it is not technically feasible here to identify in any detail the elements of this set, it is possible to consider the coherence, consistency, and relevance of the data base defined by those elements.

Coherence is judged, in part, by the degree to which it is possible to compare results in one empirical test with those in another test of the theories in the program. The greater the comparability, the more coherent the data base. By this standard the data base of the expectation states program is exceptionally coherent. Most empirical evaluations of expectation states theories are experimental in design; these experiments are most frequently performed in a standardized experimental situation expressly constructed to meet many of the scope conditions of the theories and to permit the isolation of one or another of the social processes under study.

The character of the standardized experimental setting has become much more streamlined and technical over the history of the program. Originally, data were gathered using Bales's (1950) Interaction Process Analysis (IPA). Later, categories of the IPA scheme were selected, collapsed, or redefined to form the behavioral categories that compose the observable power and prestige order. This change eventually permitted the development of the experimental situation mentioned above to control any of these behaviors (and hence to isolate or eliminate their effects). Progressively more versatile versions of this situation have followed.

Thus, additions to and changes in the techniques and procedures in the observational set have increased the coherence of the data base of the expectation states program dramatically since Berger (1957). Results from a very large number of studies can be rather easily compared. The coherence of the data base of the program is, therefore, rather high.

Of course, coherent procedures are of little consequence to a program unless a significant proportion of the data gathered using those procedures are consistent with theoretical predictions. Results in expectation states studies have generally confirmed predictions.

In the power and prestige branch at least ten experiments have been performed. Significant disconfirming results have appeared in only three of these studies, and in two of them the results were only partially inconsistent.

At least fourteen experiments have tested predictions made from theories in the status characteristics branch of the program. In only one case were the predictions not supported, and later research showed that the study had violated a central scope condition of the 1966 theory upon which the study was based (see Seashore, 1968; Cohen et al., 1969).

Although the results of these studies are all consistent with predictions, they are not all consistent with each other. The most important contradiction concerns the eliminating versus combining argument for multicharacteristic situations, with initial support for the two different predictions appearing in Freese and Cohen (1973) and in Berger and Fisek (1970), respectively. Although later results generally supported the combining argument, the contradiction has not been completely resolved and continues to generate theoretical and empirical attention.

In the distributive justice branch of the program, at least four empirical investigations have been performed. All provide basic support for the theory. However, confidence in some of these findings is limited by the possibility of an alternative interpretation based on the demand characteristics of the experimental situation.

Finally, the source branch theories have been tested in at least six separate experiments. All six provide basic support for the theories.

Overall, the data gathered in each of the four branches of the program have been quite consistent with predictions (although in the case of distributive justice the amount of data gathered has been comparatively small).

The growth of the data base has been interesting in several respects. First, in all four branches the first results to become part of the observational set were confirmatory. In general, what few disconfirmations have been added to the set have occurred much later in the history of the program and have always involved extensions not previously supported by data.

Second, in all three branches where extensive data have been gathered, early results evaluated central predictions of the theories, while later results evaluated specific alternative extensions of or derivations from these predictions. In fact, many later studies were designed to permit interpretation within the structures of the theories of *several possible outcomes*. The best example of this is Berger and Fisek's (1970) specification of both eliminating and combining arguments for multicharacteristic status situations.

Third, particularly in the status characteristics branch, theories have frequently "outrun" the experimental tests (e.g., the rapid succession of the 1966, 1974, and 1977 theories, even though significant avenues of empirical evaluation of each earlier theory remained to be investigated).

Finally, in the distributive justice branch, resolution of a problem of empirical interpretation has depended on the importation of ideas from another branch of the program—status characteristics theory. The demand characteristic problem seems to have stymied the distributive justice branch. However, the integrating theory developed by Berger et al. (1983) seems to suggest a way out of that dilemma (although, of course, that theory remains to be tested). In any case this situation demonstrates the value of having other problems in the program, other elements in the heuristic set; they may just help resolve problems in different branches.

Only one element of the observational set of the expectation states program bears on the issue of the relevance of the data base. This is the Savage and Webster (1972) demonstration that the empirical predictions in Webster (1969) cannot be validly derived from his theoretical assumptions. However, since Savage and Webster propose a relatively straightforward formalization of Webster's theory that would permit valid derivation of Webster's predictions, the criticism is moot.

To review, then, the composition and character of the observational set of the expectation states TRP indicate that the data base of the program (1) has become increasingly and exceptionally coherent, (2) is strongly consistent externally (i.e., with the specific theories tested) and relatively consistent internally (i.e., among the results of different studies), and (3) is generally relevant to the theoretical arguments it purports to evaluate. The observational set has proved a significant impetus for growth within the program.

Additional Comments

Several features observed in the anatomical growth of the expectation states program would be worth investigating in future work on TRPs. Three of these features are outlined below.

The "working out" of the core set. Much of the development in the expectation states program has served to clarify and refine the character of the core concepts and assertions. This solidification process may be a prominent feature of other programs as well, particularly early in their development.

The branching of the program through the application of particular auxiliary elements to the explanation of new elements in the heuristic set. In fact, as these branches develop, some of the auxiliary elements become core to the particular branch. It is likely therefore that program branches can be analyzed in much the same way as programs themselves.

The importance of early observational support. In those branches of the program where supportive research closely followed the formulation of the theory, later development has been much more rapid than in branches where that support (in fact, that research) has been scarce. Perhaps, with development, more alternatives for testing or for replacing falsified theories become available than are generally available earlier in a program's history. It may even be that initial supportive evidence is a necessary condition of program, or of program branch, development.

ANATOMICAL SETS AND
PATTERNS OF THEORY GROWTH

What relationship is there between the anatomy of a program and the types of relations that may occur within it? More specifically, how do the various types of relations, as patterns of theory growth, affect the composition and character of the anatomical sets?

In the case of elaboration, the effect may be quite comprehensive. Elaborations often enhance the properties of core set elements by refining or formalizing them. They also may add elements to the set (from the auxiliary set) through increases in scope. Of course, scope increases also represent changes in the character of elements already in the heuristic set. Finally, elaborations may also enhance the consistency of the data base in the observational set (especially if the elaboration is an "empirical" one), as well as the coherence of that base (if, for example, formalization permits more exact specification of the properties of situations appropriate for testing the theory).

The effects of variation are ordinarily quite a bit less dramatic. At least as long as the conflict represented in the variant theories remains unresolved, there is unlikely to be any change in the core set (although such a change may occur once the conflict is resolved). For much the same reason, there is usually no immediate effect on the character or composition of the heuristic set. Instead, changes that result from variations are usually concentrated in the auxiliary set; new concepts and assertions are generated to describe an alternate theoretical mechanism. Changes may also occur in the observational set on the basis of variation, since they often either suggest or reflect an inconsistency in the data base.

Proliferation may or may not have an effect on the core. If the core elements have not yet been clearly identified, proliferation may often help to specify them. The more a particular concept or assertion is used in dealing with different problems, the more central it is likely to be for the entire program. Of course, if the core elements have already been identified, proliferation will probably have little effect on the composition or character of the core set. However, proliferation does generally have a dramatic effect on the auxiliary set; creating a proliferation requires the statement of a large number of new ideas necessary to deal with a new explanatory domain; since most of these ideas are specific to the proliferant theory, they become part of the auxiliary set. And, since proliferation introduces a new explanatory domain to the program, it also represents an addition of at least one element to the heuristic set. Finally, proliferation is likely to decrease the coherence of the data base, since the testing situation must be less systematized to permit evaluations of theories in the new area. (Proliferation, however, does open up new areas for evidence gathering, so that the consistency of the observational set *may* increase.)

Integration has a very interesting effect on the anatomy of a program. First, integration almost inevitably increases the number of elements in the core set; in a sense, it is the clearest method by which one can identify what truly *is* core to the program. By virtue of this effect, integration is also quite likely to reduce the size of the auxiliary set; one of the prime values of an integration is that it simplifies things, allowing the elimination of excess theoretical baggage. Integrations of variants have little effect on the heuristic set. However, integrations of proliferants serve to reduce the size of that set, since two or more previously independent explanatory domains are shown to be one. Integration of competitors may have widely varying effects on the heuristic set, depending on the extent to which it incorporates the problem foci of the earlier competing theories and on the extent to which the new theoretical language it uses defines new theoretical problems for the integrating theory to solve. Since integration is similar to elaboration in many ways, its effect on the observational set is much the same; the coherence and consistency of the set are likely to be increased; the effect may even be multiplicative, since the integration performs two or more elaborations at once.

Finally, as may be expected, competition has a very different effect on the anatomy of a program. To begin with, it is likely to reduce the clarity of the core; the challenge a competitor represents strikes at the very heart of a theory. In the attempt to respond to that challenge, the theorist is likely to introduce considerable *ad hoc* reasoning, intended only to fend off the competing theory; thus, the size of the auxiliary set is likely to increase indefinitely. Further, since competitors usually do not share explanatory domains completely, and in fact may disagree over what the explanatory domain actually is, the clarity of the heuristic set is likely to suffer in competition as well. The most dramatic effect of competition, however, is reserved for the observational set. Since competitors have so little in common, almost everything about them may become a matter for debate. As a consequence, the coherence, consistency, and relevance of the data base may all be challenged. Little theoretical progress can be made as long as the challenge remains unresolved.

These comments clearly suggest that elaboration, variation, proliferation, and integration all are likely to have beneficial consequences for the anatomy of a theoretical research program—that is, to contribute to its growth. They just as clearly suggest that competition is quite unlikely to have such beneficial consequences; it simply does not contribute to program growth in any direct sense.

EVALUATING PROGRAM GROWTH

The Importance of Breadth and Density

To this point, we have dealt exclusively with theory growth *within* programs. It is reasonable, however, to discuss the growth of programs themselves. I suggest that the growth of programs should also be viewed as multidimensional. Specifically, program growth (as opposed to theory growth) involves increases in both the *breadth* and *density* of the explanations provided by the theories in the program.

Breadth refers to the range of problems, the diversity of phenomena, the variety of explanatory domains, that the program permits the theorist to explain. It describes how wide a net the program casts. Density refers to the specificity or completeness of the accounts provided for established problems in the program. It describes how fine a net the program casts.

Attempts to increase the breadth of a program seem to involve proliferation most directly; expanding the range of problems in a program is accomplished by proliferating theories in the program. Attempts to increase the density of a program seem to involve elaboration, variation, and integration most directly; refining the accounts of problems already in the program is accomplished by all three of these methods.

Increases in both breadth and density, I argue, are likely to be necessary for the continued theoretical viability of a program. A TRP must reach out to new explanatory domains and refine its accounts of old ones if it is to grow.

Clearly, our accounts of theoretical problems must improve over time if we wish to consider our knowledge to have grown or developed. However, this means much more than that our ideas should be increasingly well supported. It also implies that our theories should become more comprehensive, more precise, more rigorous, and so on. This, in turn, suggests that, even when a theory is consistent with the data, we still ought to seek to improve it through elaboration, variation, and integration. The more successful a program is in generating theories of this sort, the more powerful the program is likely to be.

Just as clearly, the variety of problems for which we can account must increase over time if we wish to consider our knowledge to have grown or developed. This also means much more than supporting our ideas empirically. It implies that the range of application of our theories should increase as well. Again, even when a theory is consistent with data, we still ought to seek to improve it, in this context through proliferation.

In some ways, breadth may be even more important for theoretical growth than is density. Increases in breadth through proliferation do, of course, bring more issues within the rubric of a program, adding grist to the explanatory mill, so to speak. In addition, increasing the breadth of a program is likely to aid in increasing its density as well. For example, problems, conflicts, or dilemmas that seem difficult to resolve may arise in a program. Alternate areas of the program, developed through proliferation, may suggest means of resolving such problems. Even when this is not possible, the presence of other program branches allows the program to continue to grow in those areas while attempts are made to resolve the problem "internally." As a consequence, a failure at one point in the development of a program does not destroy or arrest the growth of the program. Thus, the more successful a program is in generating proliferants, the more flexible the program is likely to be.

Bringing Competition Back In

Throughout this monograph I have treated competition as the weak link in the attempt to develop our theoretical knowledge. Now I wish to revise my position somewhat and argue that, under some circumstances, competition can be a relatively more valuable pattern of theoretical development.

The value of competition is based largely on its relation to proliferation. Frequently, proliferants in a program are designed as competitors with theories from other programs. Such, for example, is the case with the status value theory of distributive justice; this proliferation of the expectation states program was developed primarily to challenge the account of distributive justice provided in the equity program. Under these circumstances, the evaluation of a competitor is now tied to the development of a theoretical research program; the elaboration of a proliferant in the program is geared to the explanatory domain of a competitor. When this occurs, the outcome of the competition between the two theories is likely to depend, at least in part, on the relative breadth and density of the programs to which the competitors belong. The more powerful and flexible the program, the more powerful and flexible are the proliferants it generates to compete with other programs.

In the absence of TRPs, competing theories are likely to be quite inflexible. In general, they are unable to adapt to changing intellectual or empirical circumstances because there is no background of related work upon which to draw. Competitors in such situations are like intellectual dinosaurs. However, when competing theories are backed by TRPs, a great deal more flexibility is possible. As circumstances change, competing theories are likely to be better able to adapt to them. Therefore, they are more likely to continue to develop.

This suggests that competition might be more appropriate as a relation between programs than as a relation between theories. That is, programs compete long-term over explanatory domains. And it is that very competition that provides the impetus for the elaboration, variation, proliferation, and integration of theories within a program.

Chapter 6

The Social Context of Theory Growth

THE ISSUE

To this point we have focused most of our attention on "internal" factors involved in theory growth. We have considered differences in the kinds of theory that may grow, in the forms that growth may take, and in the character of the assessment and choice situations associated with each form of growth. However, none of this occurs in a vacuum. A variety of "external" factors also are involved in theory growth. In particular, sociological processes play as important a role in theory growth as do intellectual processes. For example, differences in the institutional resources available to a theorist are bound to affect the manner in which and the degree to which a theory can be developed.

The purpose of this chapter is to explore in general terms how such sociological processes may affect theory growth. There are at least two different ways in which this may occur. First, sociological processes may affect theory growth indirectly, through the impact that these processes have on the character of orienting strategies (which in turn influence the character of theoretical research programs). Second, sociological processes may affect theory growth directly, through the impact these processes have on the character of theoretical research programs themselves.

In this chapter I will discuss both kinds of effects. I begin with a consideration of the ways in which orienting strategies may affect the structure and development of theoretical research programs. Attention is then focused on the ways in which sociological factors may affect growth both indirectly through orienting strategies and directly through programs. Finally, I discuss the implications of the operation of both internal intellectual processes and external sociological processes on the opportunities for and the likelihood of theoretical growth.

ORIENTING STRATEGIES AND
THEORETICAL RESEARCH PROGRAMS

As I demonstrated in Chapter 2, orienting strategies have a direct and powerful impact on unit theories. They specify what problems a theory may try to solve, what conceptual apparatus may be used in constructing a potential theoretical solution, and what criteria may be employed in evaluating the worth of that solution. Clearly then, since TRPs are composed of sets of unit theories, orienting strategies ought also to have a direct and powerful impact on programs as well.

At the program level the impact of orienting strategies is most evident in the character of the anatomical sets. The most important effect is on the determination of what ideas are core to the program. The core ideas of a program are the ones that are most central and most important in its accounts of social phenomena. Consequently, these ideas are the ones most likely to be dictated directly by the strategy. For example, the notion of "reward" or "reinforcement" is core to any TRP based on an exchange strategy; its properties are defined by the conceptual structure of the strategy and its use is required by the directives of the strategy. For similar reasons the notion of "class conflict" is core to any program based on a Marxist strategy and the notion of "indexicality" is core to any program based on an ethnomethodological strategy.

Orienting strategies are less determinate in their effects on the composition and character of the auxiliary set; however, the impact is still an important one. While a strategy is unlikely to require the inclusion of any particular concepts or assertions in the auxiliary set, it may very will specify some of the properties that those concepts and assertions must manifest. In a program based on an ecological strategy, any idea that is to be incorporated in the auxiliary set ought at least to represent some material feature of the social environment. Conversely, in a program based on an interactionist strategy, any idea that is to be incorporated in the auxiliary set ought to represent some symbolic feature of the cognitive environment. Thus, while the conceptual structure and metatheoretical directives of a strategy do not require the inclusion of particular elements in the auxiliary set, the image of social reality presented by the strategy does limit the *kinds* of elements that may be included.

The effects of strategies on the heuristic set are similar in character. The heuristic set includes those problems already formulated with the concepts and assertions in the formal sets of the program. However, a strategy cannot guarantee that a particular problem will be formulated in a program; instead, it identifies what problems are to be treated as reasonable candidates for formulation. Thus, a Marxist program may formulate problems associated with social (especially class) conflict, while a functionalist program may formulate problems associated with institutional order. In general, neither strategy permits the formulation of problems outside these boundaries. Problems of conflict are the only reasonable candidates for the heuristic set in Marxism; problems of order are the only reasonable candidates in functionalism.[29]

Orienting strategies affect the observational set in several different ways. Through its metatheoretical directives a strategy may determine what kinds of data are relevant to theories in a program, what criteria are appropriate for comparing theories both within and between programs, and what kinds of research methods and techniques are to be employed in amassing data and applying evaluative criteria. Thus, in a program based on interactionism (at least of the "Chicago" variety), the metatheoretical directives dictate that data are relevant to the extent that they capture actors' symbolic definitions of social situations. This is to be accomplished by "taking the role of the other." Theoretical interpretations are valid to the extent that these others see the interpretations as matching their own. Consequently, the most appropriate research methods are those that elicit others' own interpretations of situations (e.g., relatively unstructured methods like participant and nonparticipant observation and open-ended interviewing). Again, the strategy does not dictate what data must be included in the observational set, only what kind of data (and methods of gathering it) may be included.

Through these effects on the anatomical sets, orienting strategies may also affect the patterns of growth that occur in programs. For example, through its effects on the formal and heuristic sets, a strategy may influence how each pattern is to be pursued. Only certain kinds of variants may be constructed, given the limits placed on the auxiliary set. Only certain kinds of proliferants may be constructed, given the limits placed on the heuristic set. Similarly, through its effects on the heuristic and observational sets, a strategy may influence what constitutes success at each construction task. Only some kinds of problems are worth solving and only some kinds of techniques are worth using in evaluating potential solutions.

A strategy may also influence *which* pattern is to be pursued. For instance, in programs based on phenomenology, the bulk of theoretical development seems to involve attempts to apply the same core ideas to new problem areas, to develop "social constructions" of deviance, aging, communities, and, of course, everyday reality. Thus, proliferation appears to be the pattern most preferred in phenomenological programs.

A strategy may even influence whether or not theoretical growth is to be pursued at all. Insofar as ethnomethodology requires that theory be treated essentially as metatheory (see Chapter 2), it dictates that the patterns of growth I have outlined not be pursued at all.

Although these effects of orienting strategies on theoretical research programs are powerful and extensive, they need not be conscious or explicit. Quite often a program is pursued without guidance from an established strategy. The metatheoretical foundations of such programs simply have not been made explicit yet. It may in fact be one of the functions of the development of the program to reveal those underpinnings. For example, integrations and proliferations often help to clarify what ideas are truly core in a program; therefore, they may also help to clarify the conceptual framework of the strategy that implicitly guides the program. In this sense, the features of an orienting strategy may emerge from the development of a TRP, not the other way around.

THE SOCIAL CONTEXT OF ORIENTING STRATEGIES

Orienting strategies are basically systems of values guiding theoretical and empirical work. Their emergence and continued viability are largely dependent on social context. Analysis of the processes by which strategies emerge and are maintained is primarily the domain of the sociology of science and knowledge. This is not the place, therefore, to attempt a full-scale explication of these processes and their importance for theory growth. Instead, I will simply enumerate and illustrate a variety of factors that *may* affect the emergence, content, viability, or dominance of strategies (and therefore of growth through theoretical research programs).

(1) Historical. Changes in historical circumstances are likely to have a very significant impact on what features of social phenomena are considered significant (and therefore worthy of theoretical attention). As a par-

ticular feature becomes more socially problematic, interest in understanding that feature is likely to increase. Thus, the conflict strategy of Marx emerged at a time when severe economic inequality made conflict in economic interest a particularly salient feature of British society.

(2) Cultural. Differences in the values and norms that become dominant in a society should also affect which theoretical values and norms become dominant in a discipline. Individualistically oriented strategies are more likely to become dominant in an individualistically oriented society than are collectively oriented strategies.

(3) Political. Strategy preference may also depend on what individuals and institutions have the power to implement their own preferences. Although it has never been easy to adopt a Marxist strategy in the United States, it was particularly difficult to do so during the McCarthy era, when mere familiarity with the tenets of the strategy might be cause for suspicion. Indivudals like Joseph McCarthy and institutions like the Screen Actors Guild had the power to implement their own preferences.

(4) Economic. Wealthy societies and social institutions can afford to encourage the pursuit of a greater variety of strategic alternatives than can others. This is evident in the establishment of government agencies in the United States devoted to specific social problems like mental illness and drug abuse. The mandate of these agencies is to search for solutions to the specific problem, whatever the theoretical basis for the solution. The effect of economic factors is even more evident in the narrowing of the mandates of these agencies in more difficult economic times. For example, during the recession of 1981, the Reagan administration narrowed the mandate of the National Institute of Mental Health essentially to clinical explanations of individual epidemiology; other strategies of explanation were no longer to be funded.

(5) Technological. Some kinds of theoretical work depend on the development of tools appropriate for evaluating that work. The viability of strategies that are system-oriented or multicausal (e.g., some versions of functionalism and ecology) depends in part on the development of powerful computers capable of handling the complex statistical analyses required.

(6) Professional. Disciplinary differences may affect the viability of the strategy. If, for example, the strategy is not considered sufficiently "sociological," its use may be heavily criticized. Such has been the case with reductionist strategies like the behaviorist version of exchange, which

are often evaluated as inappropriate for a sociological discipline because of their emphasis on psychological explanation.

(7) Institutional. Most of the factors I have already identified operate at the level of institutions, as well as at the level of societies. In fact, many of these factors have a more powerful impact at the institutional level, since these institutions—universities, think tanks, departments, invisible colleges, and the like—are much more immediately present in the day-to-day work of the theorist. Thus, the value biases of one's colleagues, the power and prestige of one's institution, and the economic and technological resources available from these sources should strongly affect the content and viability of orienting strategies. Only some strategies receive the institutional support necessary to ensure that they are seriously considered. The prominence of functionalism in American sociology has had much to do with the eminence of its major proponents and with the prestige of the institutions ·in which these people have been employed.

(8) Personal. The choice of an orienting strategy is also affected by the details of personal biography. Everything from where one was trained to how one was brought up may influence that choice. It is usually possible, for instance, to trace intellectual lines of descent on the basis of who one's mentors were during professional training. Interactionists ordinarily are trained by interactionists, Marxists by Marxists, and ethnomethodologists by ethnomethodologists.

This list of factors is certainly not exhaustive. Nor are the examples of the operation of these factors necessarily the best or the most accurate ones. However, that list should demonstrate clearly that a large number of different social factors do affect strategies and affect them in a large number of different ways.

None of these factors is deterministic in its effects. None of them unequivocally requires the adoption or exclusion of a particular strategy. The best evidence for this claim is the diversity of strategies available in similar societal and institutional circumstances and the similarity of strategies available in diverse societal and institutional circumstances. For example, despite the implications of many of the factors listed above, Marxism remains a viable strategy in American sociology (although it is certainly not the dominant one).

The effect of these factors are, however, universal. No strategy is exempt from them; no decision regarding strategy content or strategy choice can ignore them. Furthermore, since strategy content and strategy choice strongly affect the growth of knowledge through theoretical research programs, no account of theory growth can ignore them either.

THE SOCIAL CONTEXT OF
THEORETICAL RESEARCH PROGRAMS

Social context may also affect programmatic growth more directly. Indeed, any of the factors already outlined—political, technological, professional, or whatever—may be involved. Therefore, I will not repeat the list here. Instead, I will illustrate how one or another of these factors may affect a TRP through its anatomical sets and the patterns of growth it embodies.

Consider first the consequences of social factors for the formal sets. One way in which the content of the formal sets (especially the core set) may be affected is through limitations in the technology available for representing concepts empirically. For example, in statistically sophisticated programs (e.g., status attainment), concepts may sometimes be included or excluded on the basis of the availability of a reasonable technique of measuring the concept (or perhaps even of a data set in which that technique can be employed). Thus, the technology of research influences the content of the core set.

Economic incentives may influence the composition of the heuristic set. Some problems may become candidates for inclusion in the set because funding is available to investigate them. Certainly, the pursuit of particular problems in deviance has been affected by the establishment of government agencies to fund work on mental illness and drug abuse. Of course, economic incentives cannot determine whether the pursuit will be successful. Whether a particular candidate for inclusion in the heuristic set actually comes to be included depends primarily on other, nonsocial factors.

Some features of the observational set of a program may be affected by the availability of institutional resources. For example, if the institution provides money and other resources for the purchase of data sets and computer time but not for the purchase of laboratory equipment or the payment of subjects, survey research and secondary data analysis are much more likely to be used to test a theory than is laboratory experimentation. Since the research method used affects both the relevance and the coherence of the data base, the consequences of differential distribution of institutional resources for the character of the observational set may be quite large and widespread.

Social factors may also influence the patterns of growth in a program. One way this may occur is through the differential availability of both material and symbolic rewards for the pursuit of each type. For example, a young assistant professor, working under the pressures of the tenure system, is more likely to choose elaboration or variation than proliferation as a method of theory development. The payoff for proliferation depends on further development of the theory; no one can satisfactorily judge the value of a proliferation until such elaboration occurs. In contrast, the payoff for elaboration or variation is much more immediate; others can determine the value of the accomplishment without further development being required. In a somewhat different vein, journals seem to prefer to publish integrations over variants. Since the purposes of the latter are often nearly invisible to outsiders, while the purposes of the former are nearly always quite visible and dramatic, some reviewers are likely to see integrations as more important (and therefore more worth publishing) than variations. In addition, the prestige of a journal depends in part on the prominence of its articles. Since integrations are seen as more important, they are likely to gain greater prominence. They are doubly preferred over variants.

The same caveats apply here as in the previous section. In particular, the effects of social factors on theeoretical research programs are not deterministic; they are universal. No program is exempt from them, and no decision regarding program content or choice can ignore them.

IMPLICATIONS

Clearly, social context plays a very important role in theory growth, both directly through its effects on programs and indirectly through its effects on strategies. However, social context does not and cannot determine whether theory growth actually occurs. First, as I have already suggested, the social processes involved are not deterministic; they influence the character of strategies and programs, but they do not control it. More important, these social processes operate primarily to enhance or hinder the *opportunities* for theory growth; they have little to do with whether those opportunities are used successfully or not.

Let us consider this claim a little more specifically. Social context, primarily through its effects on orienting strategies, tell us

(1)   what kinds of theoretical structures are worth building,

(2)   what kinds of tools and materials are useful in building those structures,

(3)   what kinds of criteria we should use in evaluating the quality of the structures we have built, and

(4)   what means of revising and improving these structures are appropriate.

Social context, therefore, establishes the framework within which growth may occur. Within that framework, however, decisions are "objective" (i.e., context-independent). That is the very purpose of establishing the framework in the first place. Within the guidelines established, one can objectively evaluate success or failure in the theory construction task: Has a worthwhile problem been defined? Have the right tools and materials been used? Have reasonable criteria of evaluation been employed? Whether one has succeeded or failed is objectively determined, given the guidelines (and cannot be determined at all without them).

On this issue, at least, it might be useful to view theory growth as a game. Social context helps to establish the goals of the game and to delimit the means that may be used to achieve those goals. However, social context cannot guarantee that you will win the game; it can only show you how to determine (objectively) whether you have won.

Thus, no social context can ensure growth. Nor, in fact, can any method of theory construction ensure growth. There is no guarantee that, if one pursues elaboration, variation, proliferation, integration, and competition, theoretical knowledge will grow. I do *not* claim that pursuit of any of these objectives ensures growth. What I do claim is that *if growth occurs, these kinds of steps must be involved.*

Finally, it is important not to mistake institutional growth for theoretical growth. The amount of financing available for a particular kind of theoretical work, the number of citations of that work, the number of people who adopt the strategy on which the work is based may all increase, but none of those things constitutes theoretical growth. Ultimately, the growth of knowledge is an intellectual process. Sociological processes help shape the opportunities for that growth to occur; they neither constitute such growth nor ensure its accomplishment.

Chapter 7

Toward a Theory of Theory Growth

PURPOSE OF THE CHAPTER

As the last several chapters should indicate, developing cumulative sociological knowledge is a considerably more complex process than has traditionally been assumed. We need to know more. In a sense, we need a theoretical research program concerned with elaborating, varying, proliferating, and integrating our understanding of the process of theoretical growth itself. Toward that end I present in this chapter some guidelines regarding the kind of analysis I believe is needed—in effect, an orienting strategy for the development of knowledge about theory growth.

The strategy I propose is evolutionary in character. It draws heavily on the work of several prominent philosophers of science. In the sections that follow I first trace the roots of my evolutionary approach in the work of these people. I then outline the position I propose and relate it to these roots.

POPPER'S CONJECTURES AND REFUTATIONS

Perhaps the deepest roots of the position I propose are in the work of Karl Popper. Popper's reputation in sociology is based primarily on his scathing critique of the historicist position in the social sciences (see Popper, 1964, 1966). However, this work is but one application of a view of science that Popper has been developing for half a century (see Popper, 1965, 1968a, 1972b, 1983; see also Schilpp, 1974; Ackermann, 1976). It would be folly to attempt to review here all of this work. Instead I will focus on a few articles (Popper, 1957, 1968b, 1971, 1972a) that present the essence of his position as it relates to my work.

Popper's philosophy is rooted in his "solution" to Hume's problem of induction. Briefly, Popper's version of the problem may be stated as follows: Why do we reason from instances of which we have experience to those of which we have no experience, expecting conformity of the latter to the former, when we clearly have no logical justification for doing so? His answer is simple and direct: In fact, the problem does not really exist, for we do *not* reason by induction (i.e., from the experienced to the unexperienced); rather we reason by trial and error, or, in terms more familiarly Popperian, by conjectures and refutations.

For Popper all human knowledge is gained through the reasoning process of conjecture and refutation. We are born with at least a small set of expectations or beliefs (i.e., conjectures) about the world that are subsequently subjected to the test of experience. We retain these expectations as long as they do not conflict with experiences (i.e., as long as the conjectures are not refuted); however, when our expectations do conflict with experience, we replace them with other beliefs that do not conflict with experience. Presumably, over time we learn. That is, we arrive at expectations less frequently contradicted by experience.

What distinguishes science from other types of knowledge gathering is the systematic attempt to contradict our expectations with experience, to refute our conjectures, to falsify our theories. This at first seems an odd focus of scientific activity; one would think we should attempt to confirm our theories with experience, indeed to develop theories that cannot be falsified by experience. But, Popper argues, this is misleading, for the falsifiability of a theory is directly related to its informative content. Hence, the less falsifiable a theory, the less information or knowledge it conveys. Therefore, if we wish to accumulate knowledge we must set out not to confirm our theories, but to falsify them, to devise the most falsifiable (in Popper's terms, the least "probable") theories we can, and then to subject them to the severest tests possible. If the theory survives such tests, we have learned something, given the high information content in such a theory. If the theory fails such tests, we have also learned something—that the information contained in the theory was inaccurate and that any future theories we propose should contain different (falsifiable) information.

Note that the survival by a theory of an attempt to falsify does not make it more probable (let alone establish it as true), since our assessment of a theory depends entirely on its record of *past* performance, not on its potential *future* performance. Hence, it is never unreasonable to propose an alternative theory for testing. Further, at any point in time there may be none, one, or many theories that have survived attempts to falsify them (in Popper's terms, that have been "corroborated").

Choice, or preference, from among competing theories must therefore be based on a comparison of the degree of corroboration and the degree of falsifiability of the available theories. That theory is "better" which has the higher degree of corroboration and falsifiability. More specifically, the bases on which one theory may be preferred over another include, but may not be limited to: (1) greater precision of assertions (and survival of more precise tests of those assertions), (2) explanation of more facts, (3) more detailed explanation, (4) survival of tests the other theory has failed, (5) suggestion and survival of tests not considered or suggested by the other theory, and (6) unification of previously unrelated problems (see Popper, 1968b: 232).

Theoretical preference, however, is never conclusive. Since the assessment and choice of theories have nothing to do with future performance, the attempt to generate better theories never ends. First, the preferred theory must continue to be made more falsifiable, in order to subject it to more severe tests, which it may or may not survive. Second, competing theories may be proposed that are better corroborated, more falsifiable, or both. Thus, no matter how strongly preferred a theory may be at one particular time, it is always subject to replacement by competing theories (of which Popper [1971: 15] suggests there are an infinity).

This means that theoretical progress or growth is best characterized by the conjecture and refutation of increasingly falsifiable, yet well corroborated, theories. Progress toward truth in science is marked by the development of more precise, explanatory, detailed, corroborated, comprehensive, or unifying *theories,* not by the accumulation of *facts* in support of an increasingly probable theory.

This view of theoretical growth has led Popper in recent years to a more explicitly evolutionary model of the growth of knowledge. Popper does not intend this comparison to be merely metaphorical. He regards the process describing the evolution of knowledge as identical in form to the process of evolution of biological species. That is, Popper now argues more directly that

the growth of our knowledge is the result of a process closely resembling what Darwin called "natural selection"; that is, the *natural selection of hypotheses:* our knowledge consists, at every moment, of those hypotheses which have shown their (comparative) fitness by surviving so far in their struggle for existence; a competitive struggle which eliminates those hypotheses which are unfit [Popper, 1972a: 261].

There are, however, two important differences Popper perceives between the evolution of scientific knowledge and the evolution of nonscientific knowledge or of biological species. First, the evolution of scientific knowledge involves competition among theories, rather than among living things; when a scientific theory proves unfit, it is the theory that is eliminated, not the person who holds it. Second, while most other forms of evolution involve primarily processes of specialization and differentiation, scientific knowledge for Popper involves primarily processes of unification and integration (see Popper, 1972a: 262).

Of course, as Popper himself is aware (1972a: 267), the possibility of the explanation of the growth of (scientific) knowledge in evolutionary terms has so far only been established in principle. A number of philosophers and historians of science have proposed ways in which some portion of the general evolutionary argument may actually be applied. I will consider the ideas of three of them—Thomas Kuhn, Imre Lakatos, and Stephen Toulmin—below.

KUHN'S SCIENTIFIC REVOLUTIONS

The first two men whose ideas are to be considered here proceed from the assumption of a major flaw in Popper's argument. That presumed flaw involves the consequences of falsification for theory choice. If Popper is correct, any falsified theory must be rejected, for if our errors are not eliminated, progress cannot occur. Yet quite frequently, these men argue, falslified theories continue to be accepted; errors are often perpetuated, not eliminated. Kuhn and Lakatos each propose a different solution to this problem. The character of that solution then enables each one to develop a somewhat more specific model of the growth of scientific knowledge.

Thomas Kuhn's (1962 [1970]) work is perhaps better known to sociologists. Kuhn posits two completely different types of scientific activity—normal science and revolutionary science. These two types involve quite different assessment and choice criteria. Hence, the kind of growth each describes must be quite different.

In normal science the focus of research is on the verification, rather than the falsification, of paradigmatic theories. The failure to achieve an anticipated result, to verify one's hypothesis, reflects on the scientist, not on the theory. Inadequacy is in the quality of one's test of the theory, rather than in the theory itself. Therefore, the falsification of a theory is more likely to lead to a rejection of the theorist than of the theory; falsified theories are not in error, they are merely poorly tested.

Kuhn uses a puzzle-solving analogy to clarify the operation of normal science. Jigsaw and crossword puzzles have definite, clearly defined solutions (usually only one). There are rules limiting the nature of legitimate solutions, as well as the steps that may be used in achieving them. If the puzzle has been correctly constructed and the puzzle solver follows the appropriate steps, the solutions can be found. If a solution has not been found, it must therefore be because the puzzle was incorrectly constructed or the puzzle solver erred (e.g., in attempting to fit a piece from another puzzle into his or her own puzzle). In normal science, theoretical problems are somewhat like such puzzles. Theoretical problems have guaranteed solutions, which can be reached if the theorist has constructed the problem correctly and has followed the appropriate steps in looking for a solution. If the solution has not been found, the theorist must have erred, either in understanding the problem or in the steps used to find a solution. Therefore, it is not that the theories prove to be inadequate when falsified, but that people have inadequately understood or used them.

The analogy of normal science with puzzle solving is, however, imperfect. For in science there is, in fact, no one guaranteed solution. Each theory is bound to be in error, false in some respects. In the short run, such problems are attributed to the theorist. However, in the long run, if no resolution is found, such "anomalies" come to be attributed to the theory. Ultimately, the weight of anomalies increases to the point where the activity of normal science breaks down and that of revolutionary science begins.

Revolutionary science operates much in the manner Popper suggests for all science. That is, the anomalies in the earlier paradigm theory (i.e., its refutations) lead most scientists to reject it and, via a gestalt switch, to arrive at a new paradigm theory (a conjecture) that is immune to those anomalies (which has not yet been refuted). Then a new period of normal science begins, with the new theory as paradigmatic, until sufficient anomalies accumulate to lead to *its* rejection and replacement with still another paradigm theory. Thus, by Kuhn's argument, the evolutionary growth of knowledge by conjecture and refutation occurs only intermittently, with long periods of puzzle solving in between.

It may seem strange to some sociologists to find Kuhn described as defending scientific progress, especially evolutionary (as opposed to revolutionary) progress, but such is in fact the case. The final chapter of Kuhn's book reveals this most clearly. Kuhn does not argue that our scientific knowledge does not become progressively better; he claims only that the measure of that progress is the point from which knowledge develops (in Popper's words, "the record of past performance"), not the point toward which it is aimed (Popper's terms are "potentiality for future performance"). Further, Kuhn's description of that progress in terms of revolutions is a "political" usage of that term, designed to suggest the role of conflict among paradigm theories in growth. When this process of conflict among theories is combined with the process of selection of the fittest theories, the argument is seen to be more clearly evolutionary in character.

LAKATOS'S SCIENTIFIC RESEARCH PROGRAMS

Kuhn resolves the problem of the persistence of falsified theories by dividing scientific activity into two parts, one of which permits and accounts for that persistence. Imre Lakatos (1968, 1970) follows a somewhat different, but related, route in his analysis of research programs.

Lakatos's argument flows from his conception of what constitutes falsification. For him falsification of a theory T does not mean that observation conflicts with the theory; instead, it means that another theory T' has been proposed that (1) explains the previous success of T and (2) has excess "empirical content" over T (i.e., predicts new facts), some of which have been corroborated (see Lakatos, 1970: 116). This view of falsification means that theory assessment is always of a series of theories, not of any individual theory. Such a series of theories may then be "progressive" or "degenerating." The series is *theoretically* progressive if each new theory has excess empirical content over its predecessor; a theoretically progressive series may then be *empirically* progressive if some of that excess content is corroborated. Otherwise, the series is degenerating. Hence, the falsification of an individual theory is not even an issue of concern.

If the successive theories in a series exhibit some sort of continuity, the series is a *research program*. It is the character of this continuity that most distinguishes Lakatos's analysis. A set of methodological rules specifying what paths of research to follow (called the "positive heuristic") and what to avoid (called the "negative heuristic") divides the content of a research program into two parts. The negative heuristic establishes a "hard core" of concepts and propositions that are immune to empirical evaluation; the positive heuristic provides a "protective belt" of auxiliary hypotheses toward which empirical assessment is directed.

Since falsification applies only to programs, the primary criterion of assessment for individual theories is "verification," by which Lakatos means corroboration of excess content. Thus, as long as theoretical and empirical activity in the protective belt leads to increaasing empirical content and increasing corroboration, the program will continue to progress or grow. Only if adjustments in the protective belt fail to increase content or corroboration may the hard core be questioned and the program abandoned.

In large part this analysis is similar to, though somewhat more specific than, Kuhn's analysis. Lakatos's argument that falsification applies only to a series of theories is parallel to Kuhn';s claim that falsification applies only to the choice among paradigm theories, not to specific problem solutions within the paradigm. Also, the kind and preponderance of scientific acitvity that Lakatos suggests occurs in the protective belt is quite similar to the puzzle solving Kuhn suggests occurs in normal science. The account of the evolution of scientific knowledge is, therefore, quite similar for Kuhn and Lakatos.

There is, however, at least one major difference between Kuhn and Lakatos. Whereas Kuhn allows only one paradigm theory to appear at a time, Lakatos permits any number of research programs to operate simultaneously. As long as the protective belt of each program continues to yield excess empirical content and periodic corroboration, the program will continue to be intellectually respectable, regardless of the status of any alternative programs.

TOULMIN'S INTELLECTUAL ECOLOGY

Stephen Toulmin is not directly concerned with the problem of the retention of falsified theories. Instead, he focuses his attention on elaboration of the evolutionary character of the growth of knowledge.

The notion of an "intellectual ecology" is central to Toulmin's account of growth (see especially Toulmin, 1972: Chap. 2-4). The environment within which growth may occur is defined in terms of the set of intellectual problems that are considered worthy of solution. These problems constitute *niches* in the intellectual ecology. The character and boundaries of these niches are determined by both social and intellectual factors. Further, changes in these factors generate changes in the demands of the niches.

A variety of concepts and conceptual structures may be proposed as useful in solving the problems presented by the niches. The population of concepts available for use at any one time depends primarily on social factors, although intellectual factors are also involved.

The determination of which concepts are most useful in solving a particular problem occurs through a process of natural selection. Both competition and adaptation are involved. That is, selection is largely the result of competition among conceptual structures, with the structure that best fits the niche (i.e., provides the most adequate solution to the problem) becoming dominant in that niche. However, to some extent conceptual structures can be modified to improve their fit to the niche. Selection depends primarily on intellectual factors, although social factors are also involved.

Thus, the growth of knowledge is evolutionary. It involves variation in and selection from a population of concepts and conceptual structures in terms of their fit with the demands of niches in the intellectual ecology. Theoretical progress, therefore, is dependent on both social and intellectual context, which determine (1) what problems are to be solved, (2) what conceptual variants are available for solving the problem, and (3) what criteria are to be used in selecting the variant that best solves the problem.

As with Popper, Toulmin's argument is not intended to be metaphorical. It is not a claim that concepts are somehow like biological organisms, so that we can apply generalizations from the latter to accounts of the former. Rather, Toulmin's argument is based on the already quite general principles of an evolutionary epistemology (see Campbell, 1974). These principles must be specified in quite different ways, depending on the nature of the application. Thus, both biological evolution and theoretical evolution are concrete instances of a more abstract process.

MY ORIENTATION

In developing my strategy for analyzing theory growth, I assume the basic philosophical orientation of Karl Popper. I accept his arguments that our scientific knowledge increases via a trial and error process. That is, I assume that (1) theory assessment involves primarily the identification of error (rather than of truth); (2) theory choice is governed by the relative capacity of competing theories to eliminate known error; and, most important, (3) theory growth is essentially an evolutionary progression of more comprehensive and more precise *theories* that have so far survived efforts to find them in error, rather than an accumulation of *observations* rendering a particular theory more probable or closer to the truth.

In addition, I accept much of the content of both Kuhn's and Lakatos's attempts to flesh out Popper's argument. Clearly, the identification of error in a theory does not always lead to its elimination. Also, theoretical entities larger than individual theories (be they paradigms or research programs) do seem to play a role in the channeling of assessment into certain areas, in the actual assessment of error, and in the selection of less error-prone alternatives. I also accept much of the content of Toulmin's characterization of theory growth as evolution in terms of an intellectual ecology.

There are, however, some differences in my position. With respect to Kuhn and Lakatos, they stem primarily from my belief that it is not necessary to distinguish between normal and revolutionary science, between the hard core and the protective belt of a program, as Kuhn and Lakatos do. These distinctions serve mainly to account for the presence of falsified theories; they do so by declaring falsification irrelevant in normal science and all assessment irrelevant in the hard core. I do not believe it is necessary to reserve areas such as these for scientific knowledge that survives despite error. *All* scientific knowledge can and should be subject to the process of trial and error. In this sense my argument is more Popperian than it is Kuhnian or Lakatosian, although its details appear more similar to the arguments of Kuhn and Lakatos (especially those of Lakatos).

With respect to Toulmin, my differences stem primarily from my belief that the appropriate units of variation are theories (or perhaps even programs) and not concepts or conceptual structures. The assertions that link concepts and the scope statements that restrict their domain of application are as important in the solution of theoretical problems as are the concepts themselves. To ignore these theoretical elements is to ignore important aspects of both variation and selection. Thus, again my argument accords somewhat more with Popper than it does with Toulmin, although many of its details appear to accord more with Toulmin.

My argument is basically as follows. First, every theory we propose is composed of several different kinds of theoretical elements—concepts, assertions, derivations, statements of scope—some of which are more central or important to the theory than are others. In addition, whenever a theory is subjected to testing, a number of additional kinds of elements are introduced—observation statements, statements liking abstract concepts to their presumed concrete instances, statements of initial conditions. Again, some of these are more critical to the test of the theory than are others.

When a theory is falsified, any one or more of these elements may have led to error; and it is highly unlikely that every element in the theory contributed to the error. Therefore, it would be foolish to discard an entire theory every time it is falsified; instead, one should attempt to identify the source of the error and replace it.

The search for error is not, and should not be, random. Rather, the focus of attention generally begins with issues like the reliability (i.e., the reproducibility) of the observations and progresses "upward" toward the theory, generally moving from the less important to the more important elements. When a likely source of error is located, the theory is retested. If the theory is still falsified, the search continues, again generally moving from observation to theory, from less central to more central.

Thus, the process of falsification, search for error, and retesting may continue indefinitely before it requires calling into question important theoretical elements. Hence a falsified theory may survive quite a long time as potential sources of error less central to the theory are considered.

When a theory survives an attempt at falsification, the next step is an attempt to improve the theory (in Lakatos's terms, to increase its empirical content). This may involve, for example, making the theoretical predictions more precise, increasing the scope or complexity of the theory's account of a particular phenomenon, or broadening the range of phenomena for which the theory accounts.

The improved theory is then subjected to testing. If it is falsified, a search is begun to find the error. If the theory is not falsified, the attempt to improve the theory continues. The improvement (i.e., the growth) of a theory may also continue indefinitely; there are an infinite number of possible improvements, and the theory, however improved, is always subject to falsification.

Technically, new theories are produced by both the revision of a theory to account for error and the improvement of a theory to increase its empirical content. These theories are related by the fact that most of their elements, particularly their important concepts and assertions, are held in common. Any set of such related theories, coupled with the research testing them, constitutes a TRP.

Any number of TRPs may exist at one time. As long as the domains of explanation of any two or more programs do not overlap, the processes of assessment, choice, and growth within one program are independent of those same processes in another program.

If, however, the domains of explanation of any two or more programs overlap, assessment, choice, and growth within the program is no longer independent of the same processes in the other programs. Specifically, the theories in each program whose scope includes the overlapping domain are compared. The theory that has the most empirical content or has been better corroborated is likely to be preferred. Note that it is possible that the terms or units of comparison in any two such theories may be different. To the extent that they are different, the choice process breaks down and the assessment of the theories becomes less dependent on the content or corroboration they possess relative to the theories in other programs.

However, to the extent that comparison and assessment can be made, the less adequate theory in an overlapping domain may then be revised or improved in an attempt to reverse the outcome of the comparison. The focus of attention is first on elements needed to provide explanations specific to the overlapping domain. Again, this process may continue indefinitely, with the theories from each program competing for dominance in the overlapping domains, on the basis of content and corroboration where possible.

Whether one is talking about improvements in theories within programs or competition between theories in overlapping programs, the primary characteristic of theoretical progress is that of increasing empirical content of programs. In other words, programs tend to branch out, to expand to provide explanations for phenomena in new domains; as programs expand, the domains of more of their theories are therefore likely to overlap. The more domians over which the theories of one program dominate those of another program, the more likely it is that attempts to improve the theories in the second program will cease. If, in the rare circumstance, one program holds complete dominance over another, the growth of the second program may stop altogether. It is even possible that the theories in the second program will no longer be used at all.

However, as long as at least one theory in a program retains control over a specific domain of application, the program may recover and continue to grow. Of course, other programs may also appear to compete with the dominant program.

All of this occurs within the framework of one or another orienting strategy (although the directives of that strategy may not yet have been made explicit). The strategy dictates what explanatory domains (theoretical problems or niches) are worthy of capture, what theoretical tools (intellectual variants) are useful in pursuit of those domains, and what criteria (selection mechanisms) are appropriate in evaluating the success of theories in capturing those domains.

Thus, with Lakatos I assume that the assessment of theory occurs in the context of sets of related theories, that the focus of attention in the event of falsification is primarily on the less central or important elements of such programs, that programs may grow (i.e., be progressive) as long as periodically corroborated content increases, and that any number of programs may grow at the same time. With Kuhn I assume that programs compete over expanding domains of explanation, that such competition may in the long term establish control by a single program over an entire field of application (in Kuhn's terms, establish a paradigm), and that a dominant program is always subject to challenge and may therefore be periodically replaced.

Aside from descriptive details that are not relevant here, what I do not assume with either Lakatos or Kuhn is the presence of areas of theoretical activity exempt from the assessment process. Differences in the consequences of assessment need not be explained by positing qualitatively different kinds of science. Instead, I argue, differences in the consequences of theory assessment may be explained by differences in the theoretical contexts that generated the theory. Whether a theory was generated as a revision of a falsified theory, as any one of a number of specific kinds of improvement in the empirical content of a corroborated theory, or as a competitor with an unrelated theory influences the character of the assessment situation. Therefore, though the criterion of assessment remains the same, the consequences of its application may differ, depending on differences in the theoretical context and focus of attention.

Finally, although I do not share Toulmin's focus specifically on conceptual evolution, I do assume that the growth of knowledge is evolutionary in a relatively strict sense of that term. It occurs within the framework of orienting strategies that establish the character of the intellectual ecology: what explanatory niches are to be filled and what kinds of theories are worthy of filling them. On this basis, theories emerge in the population as candidates for selection in each of these niches. Theories adapt to ecological circumstances through the programmatic development of elaborants, variants, proliferants, and integrants. They compete for dominance in those circumstances with competitors from other programs. Strategies become dominant largely to the extent that their theories and programs dominate the available explanatory niches. However, since both social and intellectual factors are involved throughout, dominance can never be assumed to be permanent. Changing social and intellectual circumstances may alter the intellectual ecology, requiring further evolution of knowledge. Thus, the growth of knowledge is an endless process.

Chapter 8

Conclusions

REVIEW OF WORK TO THIS POINT

I have argued that science is concerned with the development of cumulative knowledge. Insofar as sociology attempts to be a science, it too is interested in the development of cumulative knowledge.

Several issues are basic in our attempts to develop such knowledge. First, how are theories (our claims to such knowledge) assessed? Second, how do we choose between theories? Finally, and most important, how do theories and theoretical knowledge grow? Traditional accounts of these processes are inadequate, basically because they are unidimensional. In most cases such accounts consider only the relevance of empirical support. In doing so, the distinctions between theory and metatheory are often ignored. More important, the context of related theory within which theory assessment, choice, and growth take place is almost always ignored.

In Chapters 3 and 4 of this monograph I have explored that context of related theory. A variety of distinct types of relations between theories were identified. Each of these types entails a different set of assessment criteria, choice situations, and theory construction tasks. As a consequence, each contributes differently to the development of knowledge. In effect, each constitutes a different pattern of theoretical growth.

These patterns of growth can be pursued collectively and systematically in the form of theoretical research programs. In Chapter 5, I identified the anatomical (i.e., structural) properties of such programs and suggested how each type of theoretical relation affects that structure. In addition, I specified how TRPs should be evaluated and how they may contribute to the development of knowledge.

However, theoretical growth does not occur in a vacuum. A great many social factors may affect theoretical growth, both directly and indirectly. I have identified some of these factors in Chapter 6. The impact of these factors is greatest in the determination of what programs have an opportunity to grow, least in the determination of whether or not growth actually occurs.

Finally, in Chapter 7, I have considered the implications of all these ideas for the development of a theory of theory growth. I proposed several guidelines for the construction of an evolutionary model of theory growth. This model is based in large part on the work of Popper, Kuhn, Lakatos, and Toulmin in the philosophy of science, although some differences have been introduced.

The analysis I have generated (particularly in Chapters 3-5) clearly demonstrates the importance of theoretical work in the development of cumulative sociological knowledge. Much more than the empirical testing of static theories is required. Theories themselves should be modified—elaborated, varied, proliferated, integrated—even when they are supported empirically.

Thus, the defining characteristic of science—in particular, of a sociological science—is theoretical. The development of cumulative knowledge in sociology is much more a theoretical than an empirical activity, although, of course, the latter is involved. The extreme importance of theoretical activity in the pursuit of cumulative knowledge suggests two additional guidelines for that pursuit.

THEORY AS THE STARTING POINT FOR
DEVELOPING CUMULATIVE KNOWLEDGE

Most sociologists have treated theory as the endpoint of the sociological investigative process. The process begins with the gathering of data, or perhaps with a rudimentary theory sketch. In either case, an attempt is then made to gather more data. A theory sketch may then result, or, if the process began with a theory sketch, that sketch may be somewhat clarified. Whatever the process by which the theory sketch has been generated, its value is determined almost entirely by its level of empirical support; if the support is strong, its value is high; if the support is weak, its value is low. Once a sketch has been determined to have at least reasonably high value, either of two things may happen to it. First, it may be treated as background knowledge that enables the theorist to test other ideas. Second, it may be retested empirically in an attempt to prove it wrong. What generally does *not* occur is a continued effort to improve the theory; there is no sense of "building" on the theoretical edifice constructed by this process.

I suggest here that theory *should* build on other theory, and that it should do so regularly. In the terms of Popper (1968b), the content of theory should increase, presenting it with ever more stringent tests of its mettle, even when data present no challenge to its legitimacy.

Sociology is often criticized for the common sense nature of most of its theories. There is nothing, in fact, wrong with common sense, particularly as a starting point for the development of ideas. There is, however, something wrong with what we do with our common sense theories. Suppose a common sense theory is tested empirically and supported; it is then accepted as a truism, as legitimate common sense. Suppose a common sense theory is tested empirically and found wanting; it is then replaced with other common sense notions not yet shown to be illegitimate. In either case, *there is no advance of knowledge.* Our understanding of the world remains at a common sense level. Clearly, therefore, something more than the generation and testing of common sense notions is required for the development of cumulative knowledge; common sense notions must be refined, expanded, modified, elaborated, developed; they must become truly uncommon sense.

This proposal is not simply a call for theoretical relevance in our data gathering, nor is it only a call for the guidance of such activity by theory. These are certainly necessary, but they are not sufficient. Rather, the proposal is a cry for some theoretical imagination. Yes, data are informative for theory, but they do not tell us everything. Data constitutes only one input to knowledge; theoretical creativity, often ignored, constitutes the other.

How, then, would I recommend that the development of cumulative knowledge be pursued? My answer involved several steps. First, begin with a theoretical idea. That idea may be generated from the metatheoretical directives of one's orienting strategy; it may be generated from data; it may in fact be generated from any source the theorist desires. Second, develop the idea. More specifically, elaborate it, build variants of it, create proliferations from it, use it to challenge competing theories. If possible, pursue these avenues of development systematically in theoretical research programs. Finally, test the idea frequently against the data; do not, however, assume that the developmental task has been accomplished if data consistently support the idea. For, in fact, the task never ends; it is always possible to improve a theory; so return to the second step and build some more.

Even these steps will not regularly generate cumulative knowledge unless one final feature is present.

THEORY AS THE STARTING POINT
FOR SOCIOLOGICAL CAREERS

Not only do we treat theory as the endpoint of the investigative process, we ordinarily treat theory as the endpoint of sociological careers. I am not sure of all of the reasons for this. Probably a major reason is an argument from "experience." Only the elder statespersons of the discipline are presumed to have looked at enough of the world (i.e., data) to theorize resonably about it. Only the elder statespersons of the discipline are presumed to have made enough mistakes from which to learn the correct path to knowledge. As a consequence, there is a tendency in sociology for theory to appear only as a magnum opus at the end of a career.[30]

These presumptions are not simply wrong; they greatly hinder the development of knowledge.

Consider the situation from the point of view of the sociology of science. One of the most basic findings in that area is that a scientist's best work (theoretical or empirical) is often done while young. Delaying theoretical activity to the end of a scientific career wastes many good years. It also tends to make the discipline intellectually quite conservative; only ideas that have "stood the test of time" are assumed to be good ones.

Consider the situation from the point of view of the development of theory. Developing a theory is a time-consuming process. Waiting until the end of one's career to start theorizing leaves little time for development. By contrast, theorizing at the beginning of one's career leaves room for pursuing *several* paths of development.

Finally, consider the situation from the point of view of training sociologists to engage in theoretical activity. Theorizing as the endpoint of a career suggests that experience is the best teacher. Exposure to a wealth of empirical data over a long period of time will reveal all; no other means will do. Thus, one must pursue something else (namely, empirical experience) in order to develop theory later. Under such circumstances it is nearly impossible to develop a tradition of theory bulding.

Yet, to pursue any of the paths of development I have identified, either individually or programmatically, sociologists must be trained to look for such things. They must have time to pursue these paths and be rewarded for that pursuit. Further, that pursuit must be a general phenomenon. Cumulative theoretical development depends on the activity of many, not on the expertise of a few. Without a general effort, the attempt to build cumulative theory becomes a personal commitment, not a disciplinary focus. Those who make the commitment work in isolation, with little opportunity to interact with others who may contribute to that development. Thus, there must be a sufficiently large body of sociologists who understand and work with theory and programs of theory throughout their sociological lives. As Berger, Zelditch, and Anderson (1972: xx) have suggested,

> [S]ociologists require a distinctive research tradition the aims, methods, and standards of which are oriented to the accumulation of general knowledge. We emphasize that it is a tradition that is required; it is not enough simply to admire a few great men who have a few great ideas. Particular extraordinary men are not a tradition nor is having ideas enough. For some sociologists generalizing must be a customary, routine, ordinary way of work; individuals must be recruited, motivated, rewarded, trained for working in this way; and its practice must be seen as not the special province only of great men, but the distinctive strategy of those committed to explicitly developing general knowledge of social behavior.

I could state the call no better.

Notes

1. Actually, as we shall see in Chapter 7, such followers are distorting Kuhn's argument. Kuhn does see scientific change as progressive. However, that progress is better described as "evolution from what we do know" (i.e., from the less articulated and specialized theories of the past) than as "evolution toward what we wish to know" (i.e., toward some sort of ultimate empirical truth).

2. Each situation is presented basically as shown on pages 17-22 of Chapter 2 in Stinchcombe's book, with only minor modifications for the sake of clarity.

3. What Stinchcombe suggests here is a logical fallacy—that of "affirming the consequent." No matter how many observations are made that are consistent with the empirical implications of the theory, it is not possible logically to derive the truth or credibility of a theory through affirmations of its consequences. At best, the "derivations" Stinchcombe suggests in Situations II and III can be "reasoned intuitions."

    To be fair, Stinchcombe is aware of the character of his argument and is intentionally fallacious (see Stinchcombe, 1968: 18).

4. See Eckberg and Hill (1979) for evidence of this confusion with respect to the use of Kuhn's "paradigm" idea in sociology.

5. Concepts and conceptual schemes do have empirical import (i.e., the potential for empirical instantiation of the concepts). Concepts are neither true nor false, but their instantiations may be.

6. Put in another way, this last assertion suggests that any source of disequilibration should be treated as exogenous to the system or as performing other functions.

7. Merton's (1968) argument for "theories of the middle range" is consistent with this directive. For Merton, the ultimate goal of theory construction remains the creation of a general theory of society. He is simply arguing that the construction of middle-range theories is an efficient intermediate step in the creation of a general theory.

8. See, for example, Turner's generally excellent discussion of sociological theory in *The Structure of Sociological Theory* (third edition, 1982). In the concluding chapters of virtually every part of the book, he argues that the theoretical position under discussion is more satisfactory as a "general orientation" than as a specific, testable theory.

9. For further discussion of this point, see Chapter 6.

10. In Merton (1957) some limits are placed on the application of the theory, although none of those limits is clearly or directly identified.

11. My analysis ignores the very real problem of operationalizing the relevant concepts; I am concerned only with testability in principle here.

12. Menzies's (1982) survey of "research theory" and "theoreticians' theory" in eight major areas of sociology provides dramatic evidence of this point.

13. See especially Emerson (1972a, 1972b) on exchange and social networks.

14. Unless otherwise specified, "theory" henceforth will be used to mean "unit theory."

15. In Chapter 6, however, I will outline some of my preliminary thoughts on this subject.

16. Technically, the claim is that society either rewards positions differentially in these circumstances or it reduces its chances of survival.

17. Homans and Adams represent this comparison in slightly different ways. Specifically, Homans assumes the comparison is interpersonal, between input ratios and output ratios for both actors. Adams assumes the comparison is intrapersonal, between input/output ratios for each actor. Mathematically, however, the two assumptions are equivalent.

18. Note that this theory also assumes that actors will distribute their winning in direct proportion to their relative "contributions" to the coalition (i.e., their relative power).

19. See Hannan and Freeman (1977: 962) for further elaboration of this point.

20. Note that if T(2) is an elaborant of T(1), then integration degenerates to simple elaboration; T(3) is an elaborant of T(2) only.

21. This is a common occurrence throughout science. For example, Newton's physical principles continue to be used quite widely—even though they have been extensively revised and deepened in Einstein's work—simply because they are much easier to apply to everyday physical problems.

22. See Freese (1980) for a sophisticated analysis of sociological cumulativeness in terms of elaboration.

23. Note the similarity here with one possible outcome of the pursuit of variant theories. The difference here is that the integrating theory goes on to suggest new ideas not in either earlier theory. Such is generally not the case with the conditionalization of variant theories.

24. This presumes, of course, that it is possible to compare competing theories by these criteria.

25. In no sense, however, do I wish to claim that the expectation states program is theoretically superior to others I might have used to illustrate my points. It is simply more convenient.

26. Influence is measured in terms of P(S), or the probability that an actor stays with his or her initial choice, given a disagreement with the other(s) over the evaluation of that choice.

27. The relation is only partial because the latter theory presents assumptions relevant only to the eliminating-versus-combining issue.

28. However, if the state of program assessment is so negative that rejection of core concepts and assertions is the only remedy left, the program has probably outlived its usefulness; theories in other programs are likely to provide better accounts of any phenomenon within the explanatory domain of such a program.

29. This is not to suggest that a Marxist program can have absolutely nothing to say about order or that a functionalist program can have nothing to say about conflict. Rather, any account that these programs may provide must treat the respective processes as residual.

30. That there are in fact some young theorists in sociology does not falsify these claims. Such odd ducks are usually treated as a breed apart or assumed to lack empirical sophistication.

References

Ackermann, R. J. (1976) The Philosophy of Karl Popper. Amherst, MA: University of Massachusetts Press.

Adams, J. S. (1965) "Inequity in social exchange." Pp. 267-299 in L. Berkowitz (ed.), Advances in Experimental Social Psychology, Volume 2. New York: Academic Press.

Alexander, J. C. (1982) Theoretical Logic in Sociology, Volume 1: Positivism, Presuppositions, and Current Controversies. Berkeley: University of California Press.

Aronson, E. (1969) "The theory of cognitive dissonance: A current perspective." Pp. 2-35 in L. Berkowitz (ed.), Advances in Experimental Social Psychology, Volume 4. New York: Academic Press.

Bacharach, S. B. and E. J. Lawler (1981) Bargaining: Power, Tactics, and Outcomes. San Francisco: Jossey-Bass.

Bales, R. F. (1950) Interaction Process Analysis. Reading, MA: Addison-Wesley.

Bales, R. F. (1953) "The equilibrium problem in small groups." Pp. 111-161 in T. Parsons, R. F. Bales, and E. H. Shils (eds.), Working Papers in the Theory of Action. Glencoe, IL: Free Press.

Bales, R. F. and P. Slater (1955) "Role differentiation in small decision-making groups." Pp. 259-306 in T. Parsons and R. F. Bales (eds.), Family, Socialization, and Interaction Process. Glencoe, IL: Free Press.

Bales, R. F., F. Strodtbeck, T. Mills, and M. Roseborough (1951) "Channels of communication in small groups." American Sociological Review 16: 461-468.

Bem, D. J. (1964) An Experimental Analysis of Beliefs and Attitudes. Unpublished doctoral dissertation, University of Michigan.

Bem, D. J. (1967) "Self-perception: An alternative interpretation of cognitive dissonance phenomena." Psychological Review 74: 183-200.

Bem, D. J. (1972) "Self-perception theory." Pp. 1-62 in L. Berkowitz (ed.), Advances in Experimental Social Psychology, Volume 6. New York: Academic Press.

Berger, J. (1957) Relations between Performance, Rewards, and Action Opportunities in Small Groups. Unpublished doctoral dissertation, Harvard University.

Berger, J., B. P. Cohen, and M. Zelditch, Jr. (1966) "Status characteristics and expectation states." Pp. 29-46 in J. Berger, M. Zelditch, Jr., and B. Anderson (eds.), Sociological Theories in Progress, Volume 1. Boston: Houghton Mifflin.

Berger, J. and T. L. Conner (1969) "Performance expectations and behavior in small groups." Acta Sociologica 12: 186-198.

Berger, J. and T. L. Conner (1974) "Performance expectations and behavior in small groups: A revised formulation." Pp. 85-109 in J. Berger, T. L. Conner, and M. H. Fisek (eds.), Expectation States Theory. Cambridge, MA: Winthrop Press.

Berger, J., T. L. Conner, and M. H. Fisek [eds.] (1974) Expectations States Theory. Cambridge, MA: Winthrop Press.

Berger, J. and M. H. Fisek (1970) "Consistent and inconsistent status characteristics and the determination of power and prestige orders." Sociometry 33: 287-304.

Berger, J. and M. H. Fisek (1974) "A generalization of the status characteristics and expectation states theory." Pp. 163-205 in J. Berger, T. L. Conner, and M. H. Fisek (eds.), Expectation States Theory. Cambridge, MA: Winthrop Press.

Berger, J., M. H. Fisek, and R. Z. Norman (1977) "Status characteristics and expectation states: A graph-theoretic formulation." Pp. 91-172 in J. Berger, M. H. Fisek, R. Z. Norman, and M. Zelditch, Jr., Status Characteristics and Social Interaction. New York: Elsevier.

Berger, J., M. H. Fisek, R. Z. Norman, and D. G. Wagner (1983) "The formation of reward expectations in status situations." Pp. 126-168 in D. Messick and K. S. Cook (eds.), Equity Theory: Psychological and Sociological Perspectives. New York: Praeger.

Berger, J., M. H. Fisek, R. Z. Norman, and M. Zelditch, Jr. (1977) Status Characteristics and Social Interaction. New York: Elsevier.

Berger, J., M. Zelditch, Jr., and B. Anderson [eds.] (1972) Sociological Theories in Progress, Volume 2. Boston: Houghton Mifflin.

Berger, J., M. Zelditch, Jr., B. Anderson, and B. P. Cohen (1972) "Structural aspects of distributive justice: A status-value formulation." Pp. 119-146 in J. Berger, M. Zelditch, Jr., and B. Anderson (eds.), Sociological Theories in Progress, Volume 2. Boston: Houghton Mifflin.

Bergner, J. T. (1981) The Origins of Formalism in Social Science. Chicago: University of Chicago Press.

Bernstein, R. J. (1978) The Restructuring of Social and Political Theory. Philadelphia: University of Pennsylvania Press.

Blalock, H. M., Jr. (1969) Theory Construction. Englewood Cliffs, NJ: Prentice-Hall.

Blau, P. M. (1964) Exchange and Power in Social Life. New Yrk: Wiley.

Blumen, I. M., M. Kogan, and P. J. McCarthy (1955) The Industrial Mobility of Labor as a Probability Process. Ithaca, NY: Cornell University Press.

Blumer, H. (1969) Symbolic Interactionism. Englewood Cliffs, NJ: Prentice Hall.

Boudon, R. (1974) The Logic of Sociological Explanation. Baltimore: Penguin Books.

Burgess, R. L. and R. L. Akers (1966) "A differential association-reinforcement theory of criminal behavior." Social Problems 14: 128-147.

Burgess, R. L. and D. Bushell, Jr. [eds.] (1969) Behavioral Sociology. New York: Columbia University Press.

Campbell, D. T. (1974) "Evolutionary epistemology.' Pp. 413-463 in P. A. Schilpp (ed.), The Philosophy of Karl Popper. La Salle, IL: Open Court Press.

Caplow, T. (1956) "A theory of coalitions in the triad." American Sociological Review 21: 489-493.

Cartwright, D. P. and F. Harary (1956) "Structural balance: A generalization of Heider's theory." Psychological Review 63: 277-293.

Caudill, W. (1958) The Psychiatric Hospital as a Small Society. Cambridge, MA: Harvard University Press.

Chafetz, J. S. (1978) A Primer on the Construction and Testing of Theories in Sociology. Itasca, IL: F. E. Peacock.

Chapanis, N. P. and A. Chapanis (1964) "Cognitive dissonance: Five years later." Psychological Bulletin 61: 1-22.

Charon, J. M. (1979) Symbolic Interactionism. Englewood Cliffs, NJ: Prentice-Hall.

Cloward, R. A. and L. A. Ohlin (1960) Delinquency and Opportunity. Glencoe, IL: Free Press.

Cohen, A. K. (1955) Delinquent Boys: The Culture of the Gang. Glencoe, IL: Free Press.

Cohen, B. P. (1980) Developing Sociological Knowledge. Englewood Cliffs, NJ: Prentice-Hall.

Cohen, B. P., J. E. Kiker, and R. J. Kruse (1979) The Formation of Performance Expectatins Based on Race and Education: A Replication. Technical Report No. 30. Laboratory for Social Research, Stanford University.

Cohen, J., L. E. Hazelrigg, and W. Pope (1975) "De-Parsonizing Weber: A critique of Parsons' interpretation of Weber's sociology." American Sociological Review 40: 229-241.

Collins, R. (1975) Conflict Sociology. New York: Academic Press.

Cook, K. S. (1975) "Expectations, evaluations and equity." American Sociological Review 40: 372-388.

Cook, K. S. and R. M. Emerson (1978) "Power, equity and commitment in exchange networks." American Sociological Review 43: 721-739.

Coser, L. A. (1956) The Functions of Social Conflict. Glencoe, IL: Free Press.

Crundall, I. and M. Foddy (1981) "Vicarious exposure to a task as a basis of evaluative competence." Social Psychology Quarterly 44: 331-338.

Cuff, E. C. and G. C. F. Payne [eds.] (1979) Perspectives in Sociology. Boston: Allen and Unwin.

Dahrendorf, R. (1959) Class and Class Conflict in Industrial Society. Stanford, CA: Stanford University Press.

Davis, K. and W. E. Moore (1945) "Some principles of stratification." American Sociological Review 10: 242-249.

Defleur, M. and R. Quinney (1966) "A reformulation of Sutherland's differential association theory and a strategy for empirical verification." Journal of Research in Crime and Delinquency 3: 1-22.

Denzin, N. K. (1969) "Symbolic interactionism and ethnomethodology." American Sociological Review 34: 922-934.

Deutsch, M. and R. M. Krauss (1962) "Studies of interpersonal bargaining." Journal of Conflict Resolution 6: 52-76.

Dubin, R. (1978) Theory Building. New York: Free Press. [1969]

Durkheim, E. (1951) Suicide. New York: Free Press. [original French edition, 1897]

Durkheim, E. (1964) The Division of Labor in Society. New York: Free Press [original French edition, 1893]

Eckberg, D. L. and L. Hill, Jr. (1979) "The paradigm concept and sociology: A critical review." American Sociological Review 44: 925-937.

Ekeh, P. (1974) Social Exchange Theory. Cambridge, MA: Harvard University Press.

Emerson, R. M. (1962) "Power-dependence relations." American Sociological Review 17: 31-41.

Emerson, R. M. (1972a) "Exchange theory, part I: A psychological basis for social exchange." Pp. 38-57 in J. Berger, M. Zelditch, Jr., and B. Anderson (eds.), Sociological Theories in Progress, Volume 2, Boston: Houghton Mifflin.

Emerson, R. M. (1972b) "Exchange theory, part II: Exchange relations and network structures." Pp.58-87 in J. Berger, M. Zelditch, Jr., and B. Anderson (eds.), Sociological Theories in Progress, Volume 2, Boston: Houghton Mifflin.

Festinger, L. (1957) A Theory of Cognitive Dissonance. Stanford, CA: Stanford University Press.

Franklin, C. W., II (1982) Theoretical Perspectives in Social Psychology. Boston: Little, Brown.

Freese, L. (1980) "The problem of cumulative knowledge." Pp. 13-70 in L. Freese (ed.), Theoretical Methods in Sociology. Pittsburgh: University of Pittsburgh Press.

Freese, L. and B. P. Cohen (1973) "Eliminating status generalization." Sociometry 36: 177-193.

Gamson, W. A. (1961) "A theory of coalition formation." American Sociological Review 26: 373-382.

Garfinkel, H. (1967) Studies in Ethnomethodology. Englewood Cliffs, NJ: Prentice-Hall.

Gerard, H. B., and G. C. Mathewson (1966) "The effects of severity of initiation on liking for a group: A replication." Journal of Experimental Social Psychology 2: 278-287.

Gibbs, J. (1972) Sociological Theory Construction. Hinsdale, IL: Dryden Press.

Glaser, B. G. and A. L. Strauss (1967) The Discovery of Grounded Theory. Chicago: Aldine.

Gouldner, A. W. (1970) The Coming Crisis in Western Sociology. New York: Avon.

Gove, W. R. (1970) "Societal reaction as an explanation of mental illness: An evaluation." American Sociological Review 35: 873-884.

Gove, W. R. (1975) "Labelling and mental illness." Pp. 35-81 in W. R. Gove (ed.), The Labelling of Deviance. New York: Wiley.

Hage, J. (1972) Techniques and Problems of Theory Construction in Sociology. New York: Wiley.

Hallinan, M. (1974) The Structure of Positive Sentiment. New York: Elsevier.

Hannan, M. T. and J. Freeman (1977) "The population ecology of organizations." American Journal of Sociology 82: 929-964.

Hanson, N. R. (1958) Patterns of Discovery. New York: Cambridge University Press.

Harvey, J. H. and G. Weary (1981) Perspectives on Attributional Processes. Dubuque, IA: William C. Brown.

Hawley, A. H,. (1950) Human Ecology: A Theory of Community Structure. New York: Ronald.

Heider, F. (1944) "Social perception and phenomenal causality." Psychological Review 51: 358-374.

Heider, F. (1946) "Attitudes and cognitive organization." Journal of Psychology 21: 107-112.

Heinecke, C. and R. F. Bales (1953) "Developmental trends in the structure of small groups." Sociometry 16: 7-38.

Hempel, C. G. (1965) Aspects of Scientific Explanation. New York: Free Press.

Hirschi, T. (1969) Causes of Delinquency. Berkeley: University of California Press.

Holland, P. W. and S. Leinhardt (1971) "Transitivity in structural models of small groups." Comparative Group Studies 5: 107-124.

Homans, G. C. (1974) Social Behavior: Its Elementary Forms. New York: Harcourt, Brace and World. [1961]

Hull, C. L. (1943) Principles of Behavior. New York: Appleton-Century-Crofts.

Hyman, H. H. (1953) "The value systems of different classes." Pp. 426-442 in R. Bendix and S. M. Lipset (eds.), Class, Status and Power. New York: Free Press.

Jasso, G. (1978) "On the justice of earnings: A new specification of the justice evaluation function." American Journal of Sociology 83: 1389-1419.

Jasso, G. (1980) "A new theory of distributive justice." American Sociological Review 45: 3-32.

Jones, E. E. and K. E. Davis (1965) "From acts to dispositions: The attribution process in person perception." Pp. 219-266 in L. Berkowitz (ed.), Advances in Experimental Social Psychology, Volume 2. New York: Academic Press.

Kaplan, A. (1964) The Conduct of Inquiry. Scranton, PA: Chandler

Kelley, H. H. (1971) Attribution in Social Learning. Morristown, NJ: General Learning Press

Kelley, H. H. and J. W. Thibaut (1978) Interpersonal Relations: A Theory of Interdependence. New York: Wiley.

Kervin, J. B. (1974) "Extending expectation states theory: A quantitative model." Sociometry 37: 349-362.

Knottnerus, J. D. and T. N. Greenstein (1981) "Status and performance characteristics in social interaction: A theory of status validation." Social Psychology Quarterly 44: 338-349.
Kornhauser, R. R. (1978) Social Sources of Delinquency: An Appraisal of Analytical Models. Chicago: University of Chicago Press.
Kuhn, T. S. (1970) The Structure of Scientific Revolutions. Chicago: University of Chicago Press. [1962]
Kuhn, T. S. (1977) The Essential Tension. Chicago: University of Chicago Press.
Lakatos, I. (1968) "Criticism and the methodology of scientific research programmes." Proceedings of the Aristotelian Society 69: 149-186.
Lakatos, I. (1970) "Falsification and the methodology of scientific research programmes." Pp. 91-196 in I. Lakatos and A. Musgrave (eds.), Criticism and the Growth of Knowledge. New York: Cambridge University Press.
Lakatos, I. (1978) The Methodology of Scientific Research Programmes. New York: Cambridge University Press.
Lakatos, I. and A. Musgrave [eds.] (1970) Criticism and the Growth of Knowledge. New York: Cambridge University Press.
Laudan, L. (1977) Progress and Its Problems. Berkeley: University of California Press.
Lemert, E. M. (1951) Social Pathology. New York: McGraw-Hill.
Lenski, G. (1954) "Status crystallization: A nonvertical dimension of social stratification." American Sociological Review 19: 458-464.
Levins, R. (1968) Evolution in Changing Environments. Princeton, NJ: Princeton University Press.
Marx, K. (1977) "The Communist Manifesto." Pp. 221-247 in D. McLellan (ed.), Karl Marx: Selected Writings. New York: Oxford University Press. [original German publication, 1848]
Mayer, T. F. (1972) "Models of intragenerational mobility." Pp. 308-357 in J. Berger, M. Zelditch, Jr., and B. Anderson (eds.), Sociological Theories in Progress, Volume 2. Boston: Houghton Mifflin.
Mead, G. H. (1934) Mind, Self and Society, C. W. Morris (ed.). Chicago: University of Chicago Press.
Menzies, K. (1982) Sociological Theories in Use. London: Routledge & Kegan Paul.
Merton, R. K. (1938) "Social structure and anomie." American Sociological Review 3: 672-682.
Merton, R. K. (1957) "Continuities in the theory of social structure and anomie." Pp. 161-194 in Social Theory and Social Structure. New York: Free Press.
Merton, R. K. (1968) "On sociological theories of the middle range." Pp. 39-72 in Social Theory and Social Structure (enlarged edition). New York: Free Press.
Miller, N. E. and J. Dollard (1941) Social Learning and Imitation. New Haven, CT: Yale University Press.
Mills, C. W. (1956) The Power Elite. New York: Oxford University Press.
Mullins, N. C. (1971) The Art of Theory: Construction and Use. New York: Harper & Row.
Nagel, E. (1961) The Structure of Science. New York: Harcourt, Brace and World.
Newcomb, T. M. (1956) "The prediction of interpersonal attraction." American Psychologist 11: 575-586.
Ofshe, R. and S. L. Ofshe (1969) "Social choice and utility in coalition formation." Sociometry 32: 330-347.

Parsons, T. (1937) The Structure of Social Action. New York: McGraw-Hill.

Parsons, T. (1954) "The prospects of sociological theory." Pp. 348-369 in Essays in Sociological Theory. New York: Free Press.

Parsons, T. and R. F. Bales (1953) "The dimensions of action-space." Pp. 63-110 in T. Parsons, R. F. Bales, and E. A. Shils, Working Papers in the Theory of Action. Glencoe, IL: Free Press.

Pope, W., J. Cohen, and L. E. Hazelrigg (1975) "On the divergence of Weber and Durkheim: A critique of Parsons' convergence thesis." American Sociological Review 40: 417-427.

Popper, K. R. (1957) "Science: Conjectures and refutations." Reprinted on pp. 33-65 of Conjectures and Refutations. New York: Harper & Row.

Popper, K. R. (1964) The Poverty of Historicism. New York: Harper & Row.

Popper, K. R. (1965) The Logic of Scientific Discovery. New York: Harper & Row.

Popper, K. R. (1966) The Open Society and Its Enemies. Princeton, NJ: Princeton University Press.

Popper, K. R. (1968a) Conjectures and Refutations. New York: Harper & Row.

Popper, K. R. (1968b) "Truth, rationality, and the growth of scientific knowledge." Pp. 215-250 in Conjectures and Refutations. New York: Harper & Row.

Popper, K. R. (1971) "Conjectural knowledge: My solution to the problem of induction." Reprinted on pp. 1-31 of Objective Knowledge. Oxford: Oxford University Press.

Popper, K. R. (1972a) "Evolution and the tree of knowledge." Pp. 256-264 in Objective Knowledge. Oxford: Oxford University Press.

Popper, K. R. (1972b) Objective Knowledge: An Evolutionary Approach. New York: Oxford University Press.

Popper, K. R. (1983) Realism and the Aim of Science. Totowa, NJ: Rowman and Littlefield.

Prais, S. J. (1955) "The formal theory of social mobility." Population Studies 9: 72-81.

Reynolds, P. D. (1971) A Primer in Theory Construction. Indianapolis: Bobbs-Merrill.

Riesman, D. (1953) The Lonely Crowd. New York: Doubleday Anchor.

Ritzer, G. (1975) Sociology: A Multiple Paradigm Science. Boston: Allyn and Bacon.

Riznek, L. A. (1977) Referential Structures and the Alteration of Performance Expectations. Unpublished doctoral dissertation, University of Toronto.

Savage, I. R. and M. Webster, Jr. (1971) "Sources of evaluations reformulated and analyzed." Proceedings of the Sixth Berkeley Symposium on Mathematical Statistics and Probability 4: 317-327.

Scheff, T. J. (1966) Being Mentally Ill. Chicago: Aldine.

Scheff, T. J. (1974) "The labeling theory of mental illness." American Sociological Review 39: 444-452.

Schelling, T. C. (1966) Arms and Influence. New Haven, CT: Yale University Press.

Schilpp, P. A. [ed.] (1974) The Philosophy of Karl Popper. La Salle, IL: Open Court.

Seashore, M. J. (1968) The Formation of Performance Expectations for Self and Other in an Incongruent Status Situation. Unpublished doctoral dissertation, Stanford University.

Shaw, M. E. and P. R. Costanzo (1982) Theories of Social Psychology. New York: McGraw-Hill. [1970]

Siegel, S., A. E. Siegel, and J. M. Andrews (1964) Choice, Strategy and Utility. New York: McGraw Hill.

Simmel, G. (1955) Conflict. Glencoe, IL: Free Press. [original German edition, 1908]

Skinner, B. F. (1953) Science and Human Behavior. New York: Macmillan.

Sobieszek, B. I. (1972) "Multiple sources and the formation of performance expectations." Pacific Sociological Reivew 15: 103-122.

Stinchcombe, A. L. (1963) "Some empirical consequences of the Davis-Moore theory of stratification." American Sociological Review 28: 805-808.

Stinchcombe, A. L. (1968) Constructing Social Theories. New York: Harcourt Brace Jovanovich.

Strodtbeck, F. L., R. M. James, and C. Hawkins (1958) "Social status in jury deliberations." American Sociological Review 22: 713-719.

Suppe, F. (1977) The Structure of Scientific Theories. Urbana: University of Illinois Press.

Suppes, P. L. (1957) Introduction to Logic. New York: Van Nostrand.

Sutherland, E. H. (1937) The Professional Thief—By a Professional Thief. Chicago: University of Chicago Press.

Tedeschi, J. T., T. V. Bonoma, and B. R. Schlenker (1972) "Influence, decision, and compliance." Pp. 346-418 in J. T. Tedeschi (ed.), The Social Influence Processes. Chicago: Aldine.

Thibaut, J. W. and H. H. Kelley (1959) The Social Psychology of Groups. New York: Wiley.

Torrance, E. P. (1954) "Some consequences of power differences on decision making in permanent and temporary three-man groups." Research Studies 22: 130-140.

Toulmin, S. (1953) The Philosophy of Science. New York: Harper & Row.

Toulmin, S. (1972) Human Understanding, Volume 1: The collective use and evolution of concepts. Princeton, NJ: Princeton University Press.

Turner, J. H. (1975) "A strategy for reformulating the dialectical and functional theories of conflict." Social Forces 53: 433-444.

Turner, J. H. (1982) The Structure of Sociological Theory. Homewood, IL: Dorsey Press.

Turner, J. H. and A. Maryanski (1979) Functionalism. Menlo Park, CA: Benjamin/Cummings.

Wagner, D. G. (1978) Theoretical Research Programs: The Growth of Theoretical Knowledge in Sociology. Unpublished doctoral dissertation, Stanford University.

Wagner, D. G. and R. S. Ford (1983) "The confirmation and disconfirmation of women's status expectancies." Unpublished manuscript under review.

Wallace, W. L. (1971) The Logic of Science in Sociology. Chicago: Aldine.

Walster, E., E. Berscheid, and G. W. Walster (1973) "New directions in equity research." Journal of Personality and Social Psychology 25: 151-176.

Webster, M., Jr. (1969) "Sources of evaluation and expectations for performance." Sociometry 32: 243-258.

Webster, M., Jr., and J. E. Driskell, Jr. (1978) "Status generalization: A review and some new data." American Sociological Review 43: 220-236.

Webster, M., L. Roberts, and B. Sobieszek (1972) "Accepting significant others: Six models." American Journal of Sociology 78: 576-598.

Webster, M., Jr. and L. F. Smith (1978) "Justice and revolutionary coalitions: A test of two theories." American Journal of Sociology 84: 267-292.

Webster, M., Jr. and B. I. Sobieszek (1974) Sources of Self-Evaluation. New York: Wiley.

Willer, D. and J. Willer (1973) Systematic Empiricism: Critique of a Pseudo-Science. Englewood Cliffs, NJ: Prentice-Hall.

Winch, P. (1958) The Idea of a Social Science. London: Routledge & Kegan Paul.

Zeitlin, I. (1981) Ideology and the Development of Sociological Theory. Englewood Cliffs, NJ: Prentice-Hall.

Zelditch, M., Jr., P. Lauderdale, and S. Stublarec (1975) How Are Inconsistencies Between Status and Ability Resolved? Technical Report No. 54. Laboratory for Social Research, Stanford University.

Zetterberg, H. (1965) On Theory and Verification in Sociology. Totowa, NJ: Bedminster Press.
Zimmerman, D. H. and D. L. Wieder (1970) "Ethnomethodology and the problem of order: Comment on Denzin." Pp. 285-298 in J. Douglas (ed.), Understanding Everyday Life. Chicago: Aldine.

Index

Ackermann, R. J. 117
Adams, J. S. 39-41, 41n, 54, 65, 66, 84, 89
Akers, R. L. 46, 49
Alexander, J. C. 9
anatomical sets 90, 108, 131: auxiliary set 90-91, 93, 100-102, 108-109; core set 90-93, 91n, 97, 100-102, 108, 110, 113; heuristic set 93-95, 97, 100-102, 109, 113; observational set 95-102, 109, 113
Anderson, B. 84, 89, 93, 135
Andrews, J. M. 48
Aronson, E. 17
assessment of programs, criteria of 103-104, 126
assessment of theories 10, 12, 15-20, 23, 26, 29, 34, 37, 63-66, 115, 127, 128, 131
assessment of theories, components of: indicators 18, 126; initial conditions 126; observations 9-16, 19-22, 30, 126
assessment of theories, criteria of: comprehensiveness 39, 70, 77, 94, 119; credibility 12-15, 20-22; definitional adequacy 27, 91; depth 71; empirical support 10, 15-18, 22, 27, 35, 39, 66-76, 91, 96, 97

132-133; fertility 69, 77; logic 11, 12, 12n, 15, 30, 31, 91; parsimony 55; precision 17-22, 32, 39, 42, 64-67, 75, 77, 87, 119, 126; range 17, 19, 22, 91, 94, 126; rigor 17-22, 39, 65, 66, 69, 77, 87; scope 17-22, 31, 32, 42, 56, 64-67, 75, 91, 94, 101; simplicity 55, 65, 66, 69; statistical criteria 16, 21; systematic import 27; testability 26, 31, 32, 35, 65

Bacharach, S. B. 51-54, 70, 72
Bales, R. F. 27, 80, 81, 98
Bem, D. J. 17, 59, 74
Berger, J. 80-84, 87-89, 93, 98, 99, 135
Bergner, J. T. 9
Berscheid, E. 54
Blalock, H. M., Jr. 10, 25
Blau, P. M. 51
Blumen, I. M. 42
Blumer, H. 76
Bonoma, T. V. 46, 51
Boudon, R. 10
Burgess, R. L. 46-49

Campbell, D. T. 124
Caplow, T. 45, 67
Caudill, W. 82

About the Author

DAVID G. WAGNER is an assistant professor in the Department of Sociology at the University of Iowa. He received his B.S. in sociology from Michigan State University and his Ph.D. from Stanford University in 1978. He has previously taught in the Department of Sociology at Erindale College, University of Toronto. In addition to his work on theory growth, he is also interested in distributive justice and expectation states processes. He has recently published articles on expectations for reward in status situations, the labeling of mental illness, and the development of the expectation states theoretical research program.